# Pray Your Way

Centre for
Faith and Spirituality
Loughborough University

# Pray Your Way

*Your Personality and God*

BRUCE DUNCAN

DARTON·LONGMAN+TODD

First published in 1993 by
Darton, Longman and Todd Ltd
1 Spencer Court
140–142 Wandsworth High Street
London SW18 4JJ

Reprinted 1994, 1995 and 1998

ISBN 0–232–52019–4

A catalogue record for this book is available
from the British Library

Scripture quotations are taken from The Jerusalem
Bible and the Revised Standard Version

Cover design by Leigh Hurlock

Phototypeset by Intype, London
Printed and bound in Great Britain by
Redwood Books, Trowbridge, Wiltshire

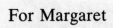

For Margaret

# Contents

# Acknowledgements

Thanks are due to the following for permission to quote copyright material: James MacGibbon, from *The Collected Poems of Stevie Smith*; W.W. Norton & Company Ltd, from *Selected Poems 1923–1958* by e.e. cummings.

# 1

## Companionship with God

*God is the great companion. He is the sufferer who under-
stands.*                                    *(A.N. Whitehead)*

At primary school we prayed daily. I remember the no-nonsense
voice of the teacher, 'Hands together, eyes closed', ruler at the
ready to rap the knuckles of any child who fidgeted or peeped.

Prayers were said. God was spoken to. Words were repeated
parrot-fashion. A few minutes later, with eyes open and hands on
head, we would chant our multiplication tables. Both experiences
were, for me, totally devoid of any real meaning. Learning multiplication tables by rote at least had the merit, with which I could
vaguely connect, of fixing in my little brain some knee-jerk
responses – eight sevens are . . . 'fifty-six!' – handy for the mental
arithmetic required before the advent of the pocket calculator.

The ritual saying of prayers in my primary school was for me
and, looking back, probably for most of my teachers also, an
unconnected and pointless ritual. I can see how it could have so
easily inoculated me for life against the possibility of catching
religion.

My childhood experience of religion in school happened in the
bad old days. That sort of thing does not happen today. Or does
it? An adult with responsibility for worship in school assemblies
may put an enormous amount of time and effort into producing
something really good, meaningful, relevant; but the children may
see it in a different light, as tiresome, preachy and hypocritical.

Worship in state schools in the United States of America is
against the law (though I was delighted to read on a school staff
notice-board in California, 'The rule forbidding praying in class
does not apply in the case of nuclear attack'). Yet a recent poll
indicates that nine out of ten American adults pray often and
regard prayer as a very important part of their lives. In Britain,
however, where acts of worship in schools are mandatory, over 60

per cent of adults claim that they never pray at all. Perhaps that is
not a surprising response if most British people in their formative
years come to think of prayer as that formal, empty 'saying prayers' that I experienced daily in primary school.

My first experience of real prayer was of simple, silent response.
It happened one Christmas time, when I was about eleven years
old. Apart from occasional and reluctant attendance at Sunday
School in the local Gospel Hall, church-going played no part in my
upbringing. But on that particular Christmas, for no fathomable
reason other than a direct prompting from God, I felt impelled to
go to church. The church I found, a couple of miles from my home,
was not a particularly attractive building, red-brick, Victorian,
empty and smelling of polish, damp, and dusty hassocks.

I remember sitting there for a long time, perfectly content,
knowing that I had to be there but not knowing why. Eventually
the vicar arrived. Seeing a small boy sitting in the nave, all alone
among the rows of empty pews, he came over to me and asked
what I was up to. I told him I was waiting. 'What are you waiting
for?' he inquired. 'For the service,' I replied. 'But it's hours before
the service,' said the vicar. 'That's OK,' I said. 'I'll wait.' And wait
I did, simply glad to be there, not knowing why.

As an adult reflecting on the powerful significance of that experience for an introverted, intuitive and very sensitive child, who was
a loner, I can see that it was a tailor-made gift of love from God to
me. All I had to do was respond, accept, say 'Yes' – and there I
was, in a relationship which I now know was prayer. From that
moment on, emotionally and experientially if not intellectually, I
knew that real prayer is our response to God's love.

As self-centred creatures, it is difficult for us to abandon the
idea that prayer is first and foremost a human activity. We think
that to pray we have to do something. We slip easily and often into
the attitude that at the end of the day prayer depends on us. We
say our prayers. We listen to God. We become aware of God's
presence. We give up some of our time to God. So often we find
ourselves behaving as if our part is to pray as we have been taught,
at set times and in set ways, with effort and discipline, while God's
part is to listen and, we hope, act in response to our prayers.

## God's Initiative

My childhood experience of genuine prayer is a constant reminder to me that the initiative is always God's, never ours. Christian prayer is a response, not a pursuit. Our prayer is *always* response to God's prayer.

If you have become used to thinking of prayer as a merely human activity, the thought of 'God's prayer' may seem strange to you. If that is the case, think about Jesus, communing with his Father, listening, speaking, healing, rebuking; acting in the whole of his ministry, the whole of his life, in an unimaginably close relationship of love to the One who sent him. 'My food,' he said, 'is to do the will of him who sent me'.[1]

The relationship between God the Father and God the Son is a relationship of prayer. 'I will pray the Father,' Jesus promised, 'and he will send you another Comforter who will be with you always. . .'[2] The Holy Spirit, God in action, infusing our lives with love, guiding, leading, prompting, encouraging us, is in a relationship of prayer with God the Father and God the Son. 'Mankind thinks it prays to God; it is not so, for prayer itself is the Divine.'[3]

When we pray we are entering a relationship of love that we call the Holy Trinity, an eternal prayer relationship in the very being of God. The God we strive towards and struggle to know and to serve is already with us, giving us the grace and the desire to pray.

The truth that our prayer is a gift from God does not mean that discipline, struggle, effort, failure and at times despair play no part in it. We can again look at our Lord's life of prayer and see it as strenuous, disciplined and purposeful. It included times of confusion, distress, anger, desolation and, as he was dying in agony on the cross, a terrible sense of abandonment by God. As we come to trust God's love, as Jesus did, so gradually we give up the pointless aspects of our struggling, our efforts to achieve in our own strength what God holds out to us as free gift, and we learn to relax with the One who alone makes it possible for us to pray in the first place.

## Growing in Prayer

In my teens, through the happy days of my secondary schooling, I was often to discover God meeting me, unexpectedly, joyfully. He

encountered me through the architecture and atmosphere of the
great cathedral church that served as our school chapel, through
the absorbed stillness of the Blessed Sacrament chapel, through
the grandeur and power of the organ music and the calm beauty of
choral evensong.

My journey led me in adolescence through gloriously eccentric
but shamefully intolerant excesses of extreme Anglo-Catholicism,
with its appeal to the senses, colour, incense, candles, vestments,
saints and shrines. The path turned to a more austere and disciplined Prayer Book Catholicism, with the divine office, sacramen-
tal confession, structured meditation, beautifully choreographed
liturgy, devotional addresses at compline, and the realisation that
God is love, even if love is not necessarily God.

Forty years further on, I can trace in those early years the beginning of a personal prayer relationship which has continued to
change and unfold with every fresh apprehension of God's grace.
It has not been an easy or automatic progress, like steadily ascend-
ing a ladder rung by rung. That metaphor of ascent, the idea that
we progress stage by stage to ever higher levels of holiness (and
therefore, by implication, ever further from this wicked world)
accords neither with my experience nor with my conviction that
the material creation is fundamentally good. Only by engaging
with God's good world, not by escaping from it, do we discover
the raw materials for holiness.

Perhaps a better metaphor for the developing prayer-relationship is that of pilgrimage or journey. One of the loveliest Gospel
stories is of Jesus, after his resurrection, joining two friends on
their walk to Emmaus.[4] In a similar way, God is our companion on
the way. He never leaves us. God is always with us on our journey
of prayer, though we do not always recognise him.

We have some maps to help us along the journey, handed down
through two millennia of Christian experience. The Church's traditions of spirituality are enormously helpful, but they are only
rough guides to our individual journeys. No one's pilgrimage of
prayer follows a fixed, prescribed route. There are thousands of
different paths. In retreats, workshops and a ministry of spiritual
direction I have been privileged to listen to many hundreds of
people talking about their own journeys of prayer. Time and again
the same features crop up in their descriptions. One of the most
common, and it is one which I know well from my own experience,
is a general sense of dissatisfaction with 'saying my prayers' or
with 'my prayer life'. Alongside that feeling of dissatisfaction is

a longing for the closer walk with God, which William Cowper described in his famous hymn. They say with St Augustine, 'Our hearts are restless, Lord, until they find their rest in you'; and they echo the yearning cry of the psalmist, 'As a doe longs for running streams, so longs my soul for you, my God. My soul thirsts for God, the God of life.'[5] They know that the love of God is the purpose, the direction and the end of their lives, and they want to express that by praying better.

Let me give you an example. A woman in her late thirties recently described to me her experience of a growing prayer-relationship with God. She wrote,

> In the last three to four years, I began to want to pray, and to pray differently. I started to feel a lack of something, and a need to be alone, silent, away, in order to focus on Christ. I went on a six-day directed retreat last year, which was quite amazing and seemed to change my life in an interior way. Previously I had once felt very overwhelmed by God's presence. The retreat was different. It was like becoming still in myself, and living with a sort of awareness of God but also a sense of not being with God, desiring him but also not desiring. Afterwards I felt an absolutely horrible blankness and sense of being abandoned. Since then I have felt 'high' and then quite blank, in a desert. Now my relationship with God is more one of faith, because I come up against the blankness, not understanding, not knowing, and find that hard. Quite often I definitely don't want to pray at all, but part of me does want to.

## Difficulties with Prayer

You have probably picked up this book because you share something of that woman's experience. You want to pray, and to pray differently. You know that ambivalence about prayer, the desiring but also not desiring. Perhaps the methods of prayer you were taught and have tried to follow for many years have become more of a dry duty than a source of joy and peace. Religious practices that had the power to sustain and encourage you may have become boring and lifeless. You too may feel abandoned by God, who once felt so very close. If at least some of this rings true, I hope you will take comfort in the knowledge that you are in no way unusual.

It must be said that our problems with prayer are often our own fault, the result of deliberate disobedience, of 'the sins that made Thee mourn and drove Thee from my breast.'[6] We experience judgement, we are convicted of sin, or we come face to face with an aspect of self-knowledge that we were deliberately trying to ignore or avoid. In this case the only way to renew our prayer-relationship is to turn and face God with honest repentance.

However, what we perceive as difficulties may not be our fault at all but the Holy Spirit's way of urging us along. There are necessary growing pains in prayer, times of dryness, darkness, boredom when all we can do is carry on in blind faith. One particular growing pain that comes to many Christians, especially during mid-life, is the need to discard or move beyond religious practices that we have outworn or that have become idols. We know that if we cling to them they will impede our progress. Habits, rituals, forms, religious practices that previously pointed the way for us and were helpful, must be sloughed off. That can be very distressing and may appear to us or, we fear, to others, as disobedience or faithlessness. It takes considerable courage to stand back, review and maybe shed a habitual, comforting piety that is not bad in itself but over the course of time has become for us a lifeless form. As we leave the form behind us and move beyond it, we are able to return to the reality with new freedom, peace and joy. In time people often return to the old form, which will then be invested with new meaning. Or new structures and habits will appear, which in their turn will have to go when they have served their purpose.

So we must learn to sit lightly to methods, rules, structures, disciplines. Helpful though they may be, they are always provisional and we should never confuse them with the underlying reality of prayer.

Clergy, who are expected to know about prayer and teach lay people how to pray, often themselves find prayer difficult. A friend of mine who is a deacon in the Church of England went through a desolate experience of abandonment by God. It lasted for many months, but in retrospect she could see that what she had suffered was a gift from God, a necessary prelude for a new, closer, more childlike, less childish, more mysterious and much less explicable prayer-relationship with God. Readers who are ordained will recognise how hard it was for her, during that tunnel-like sense of God's absence, to continue in ministry as if nothing had happened – preaching, leading worship, counselling and encouraging others in prayer. A Roman Catholic priest once described a similar experience to me as going into autopilot, just living in the clerical persona and going through the motions. Thank God the grace of holy orders is no immunisation against the growing pains of prayer. But when those pains come, clergy need understanding people around them if they are not to become locked on autopilot. They need the support of shared ministry, and the opportunity to go away, on holiday, retreat or sabbatical.

Anyway, as we will see later on, clergy, and probably most authors of books about prayer, tend to fall into a narrow and fairly unusual cluster of personality types. Ways of praying that come easily and naturally to them may not come nearly as easily or naturally to most of the population. Paradoxically, their efforts to teach people to pray may result in undermining people's natural ability for prayer. Many people are made to feel incompetent and guilty because they cannot pray as they have been taught and as they think they ought.

All our difficulties with prayer are signs of hope. They signal opportunities for new growth in our God-given life. That growth is not limited to 'the spiritual life' or the 'prayer life', as if they could have any separate meaning or existence, but is a new integration of all that has gone before in our whole life. Growth in the prayer-relationship is a movement towards a more complete formation of Christ in us,[7] which is the measure and the goal of genuine human maturity.

## Life-giving Prayer

Christian preaching and books about the spiritual life often give the impression that prayer is an unusual and rarefied activity, taken seriously only by religious people and not really belonging to the fabric of life as it is normally lived by ordinary people.

Prayer has everything to do with life, and with every part of life. It has nothing to do with limiting us, or making us feel guilty or inadequate or trapped. We must explode our narrow, falsely pious attitude to prayer into the realm of the ordinary. 'I have come so that they may have life and have it to the full,' Jesus proclaimed.[8] The life God offers to us with boundless generosity, fullness of life, *is* prayer.

Life is about loving and being loved. It is God who loves us into life. At every moment of our existence God holds us in being, breathing life into us. Prayer is that life-giving relationship with

God our Creator-Redeemer-Sanctifier. There is no moment of life when we are outside that relationship, though of course there are many times when we are unaware of it or deliberately avoid it.

Our part in prayer is to become increasingly aware of our God-relatedness. As we learn to do that, with all the will and discipline that is required, we come to share more and more freely, willingly and responsibly in the love-relationship between humanity and God, which is ultimately what life and prayer are all about.

From our human perspective, we say that we are praying when we are consciously aware of our relationship with God and deliberately attending to it. As you become increasingly conscious of your relationship of love with the Creator-Redeemer-Sanctifier God of Christian faith, so you are growing in prayer. That growth is nourished by the sacraments, corporate worship and the various duties of church membership and disciplines of Christian spirituality.

It is so sad that the common understanding of prayer is limited to special religious and verbal acts, when in truth it is such a natural and instinctive part of what it means to be human. The natural, human longing for God is frustrated by a limited understanding of prayer and of how one can or should pray. Prayer has been described in dozens of ways, such as 'a familiar conversation with God', 'friendship with God', 'the lifting of the heart and mind to God'. Our limited ideas about the nature of prayer must be exploded to include all the familiar definitions without being confined by them.

All ordinary human longings for happiness, every spontaneous response of love and joy, every striving towards goodness, every impulse to serve, our sense of guilt and sorrow – all this, and more, is prayer. If only we can learn to recognise as true prayer the soul's sincere desire, uttered or unexpressed, the people who say they never pray can be brought to recognise where prayer is already in their lives. Instead of feeling divorced from the whole religious enterprise, or guilty about not praying, they can be immensely encouraged by recognising that they pray much more and probably far better than they ever imagined.

## Prayer and Personality

Some people are very suspicious about the current surge of interest in spirituality and personal development. They see it as self-indulgent and narcissistic, a symptom of individualistic, privatised religion.

There has always been a creative tension in Christian living between praying and doing. For some the Christian life is primarily concerned with Christian action in the world. For others, prayer is primary. The tension is well illustrated by the story of Martha and Mary. 'Martha, Martha', Jesus said, 'you worry and fret about so many things, and yet few are needed, indeed only one. It is Mary who has chosen the better part; it is not to be taken from her'.[9] Sitting at Jesus' feet, listening to the Word of God, is the better part. Attending to God must always come first, but it must also bear fruit in terms of practical love and service. William Temple pointed out that most people think that conduct is what matters and prayer helps it, whereas the truth is that prayer is what matters and conduct tests it. Prayer changes us. We cannot grow in prayer without growing in social and political awareness and a desire to do our part for the coming of God's Kingdom on earth.

Prayer is the impulse of God's grace, urging and helping us to respond to the Spirit of love. As we make that response, so we lay ourselves open to being changed, to growing in thoughts, words and deeds of love. The widespread longing in the hearts of people for a closer walk with God will bear fruit. Far more dangerous than a so-called privatised spirituality is political activism that is not accompanied by any conscious connection with God.

## Prayer Unites

Prayer draws people together. That is true in several senses. When Christians of differing traditions and denominations have the will and the courage to become vulnerable to each other and to God in intimate and open prayer together, they are drawn into a unity of love that transcends ecclesiastical and doctrinal divisions. Prayer draws people together ecumenically.

It is true of intercessory prayer. Those who pray for others are drawn together by God's love, across space and time, with those for whom they pray.

It is also true of our individual lives, that prayer draws our personality together. My divided and fragmented self comes together as I turn to face the love of God in prayer. I discover more about my real identity and learn a new self-awareness as I respond to the God in whose image I am created. That is my experience, and it is echoed by all those who have shared their experience of prayer with me.

In prayer our lives become more integrated, more purposeful, and filled with new meaning. In prayer we accept the gift of God's unconditional love and total acceptance of us, just as we are. Through prayer we learn to accept, value and love ourselves. As this happens, our prayer becomes more genuine. There is a less anxious, more confident relationship between the unique self and the God who creates and enjoys us. Increased self-knowledge, with the self-assurance that says, 'It is good to be me', moves us towards a new integrity and authenticity in our approach to God.

In the power of prayer we can face our shadow side, that unconscious part of ourselves, the realm of hidden, dark and powerful energies, so difficult for us to acknowledge or understand and yet so full of life-giving potential.

## Prayer and Personality Type

The Myers-Briggs Typology Indicator® (MBTI™)[10] helps us to recognise and appreciate the psychological preferences which are the dynamic of our personalities. Discovering your own personality type can be powerfully liberating. It can unlock the door to a new adventure in self-discovery and point you to new ways of relating to God. It may illuminate hidden strengths and uncover previously unacknowledged potential in yourself. It may help you to understand and explain to yourself the touchy, vulnerable and weak aspects of your personality. It may give you the desire and confidence to explore your relationship with God in ways where you have said, 'I couldn't do that; that's definitely not for me!' If you are hoping that knowledge of your personality type will lead you to a prescribed method of prayer which will be just right for you, then I fear you may be disappointed. A dogmatic approach of the influence of psychological type on any individual's spirituality is naïve and unhelpful. The reported prayer experiences of hundreds of people, covering the whole spectrum of personality types, indicate that the connection between prayer and personality type is subtle and best understood in a descriptive and suggestive way rather than a prescriptive one.

There is, after all, much more to prayer than psychological preference. An individual's relationship with God depends entirely on the grace of the Holy Spirit. It is a mysterious relationship of love that knows no bounds. Each human being is limited by his or her individual personality. God respects our unique individuality and never violates it; but God is of course in no way limited or predicted by personality type. It seems that the one prediction we can make with confidence about God's relationship with us is that it is unpredictable.

Prayer, then, is a loving, enjoyable, fulfilling and demanding relationship which changes and develops throughout life. For the Christian, prayer is nothing less than the whole of life, committed to God and lived out, consciously and unconsciously, in the power of the Holy Spirit in union with Jesus Christ and to the glory of God the Creator.

In the pilgrimage of prayer, God tends to move us along by going with, and not against, the grain of our individual personality type. The more you know yourself, the more you will be free to recognise God's continual initiatives and respond to them by praying *your* way through life – that is, making your whole life prayer, and learning to do that as you can, and not as you can't.

# 2

# Your Personality – A Model

There are many people including sadly many professing Christians, who go through life with a depressing sense of low self-esteem. They have come to believe that they are somehow inadequate and deficient in their personalities and so spend their time looking longingly at other people, wishing they were like them. There are others who seem to be convinced that this world contains only two types of people – those who are like themselves, and those who are wrong.

One reason why I enjoy leading Myers-Briggs workshops is that the participants are so often helped to see themselves in a new light. They come to appreciate themselves as gifts from God. What this person wrote after a workshop sums up the experience:

> I've always had low self-esteem – felt that people don't ever like me for what I am, only for what I do for them. When I saw my MBTI profile I couldn't believe it. If I could have chosen to be one of the sixteen types, that is the one I would have chosen – all that I have ever wanted to be. Then I realised, that is how God has made me. Thank you God for making me me. It is the biggest liberation I have ever experienced. I didn't want to come to this workshop, but I felt the Holy Spirit giving me a kick. . .

There are as many different types of human personalities as there are human beings. The finger of God never leaves identical fingerprints. No other person in the world is quite like you. Your physical and psychological make-up, combined with your cultural background, upbringing, education and all your life experiences, make you the unique person you are.

You have certain abilities, interests, talents and tastes and you belong to a society that either provides or denies opportunities for these to flourish. Furthermore, the unique person who is you is always on the move, changing, developing, diminishing or growing.

The similarities you share with all other human beings can be listed and categorised. People can be divided and subdivided according to such factors as ethnic origin, IQ, socio-economic status, religion, and political affiliation.

Many attempts have been made to distinguish and accurately categorise the various personality types. In ancient times, astrologers classified people according to the four elements, earth, air, fire and water, and their corresponding zodiac signs. In the second century AD the Greek physician, Galen, developed a typology based on bodily secretions and we still describe people in his terms: sanguine, choleric, phlegmatic, melancholic. Earlier this century Ernst Kretschmer, followed by W.H. Sheldon, related temperament to physical characteristics. They claimed a correlation between fatness (endomorphy) and a sociable, jolly temperament called *viscerotonia*; between the bony, sinewy, athletic types (mesomorphs) and an aggressive, self-assertive temperament, *somatonia*; and between the thin types (ectomorphs) and a self-conscious, shy, intellectual temperament, *cerebrotonia*.

## Jung's Theory of Psychological Type

The typology used in this book derives from the Swiss psychologist, Carl Gustav Jung. His theory of psychological types, published in 1921, is based on distinguishable habitual preferences of thought and behaviour. The difference between Jung's theory and all other attempts to classify personality is that he focused on the inner dynamics of human life and recognised that each individual is a unique and mysterious person.

Jung described his theory as a compass, an instrument that can help us orientate ourselves in the psychological world. Properly used, it can help us to see where we are and where we should be going and it can point us along our journey towards that maturity of personality that he called 'individuation'.

## Jung's Compass

The cross of Jung's compass is made up by two fundamental human processes, that he called **perceiving** and **judging**.

```
                             P
                             E
                             R
                             C
                             E
        J U D G I N G
                             I
                             V
                             I
                             N
                             G
```

Whenever we are awake we are either gathering data (perceiving)
or we are dealing with it (judging). We are either becoming aware
of information, of ideas, people, things, happenings; or we are in
some way handling that information by forming opinions, making
decisions, reaching conclusions.

The perceiving process makes us aware of the existence of
things. This just happens, without any conscious effort or decision
on our part. Jung therefore described it as an **irrational process**.
You notice a fly buzzing on the window pane. You hear the siren
of an ambulance blaring in the distance. You become aware of a
pain in your right shoulder. Out of the blue an idea or possibility
strikes you. Thousands of similar perceptions occur to each of us
every waking hour. Much of our time is spent in the perceiving
process, gathering information, taking in data, becoming aware of
objects, ideas, and possibilities.

The judging process has nothing judgemental about it. It simply
describes the way we handle data. You listen to an argument,
weigh the evidence and come to a conclusion. The clouds look
threatening and so you take your umbrella with you. You look at
the menu and decide to order soup rather than the prawn cocktail.
You help a friend choose a new dress, one that really suits her.
Hundreds of similar judgements are made by each one of us every
day, by our judging process. Jung called it a **rational process**
because we use it consciously and intentionally, to form opinions,
come to conclusions and make decisions.

## The Four Mental Functions

At the four points of Jung's compass are the four mental functions. The opposing poles of the perceiving process are **sensing and intuition**. They are called the perceiving functions. The opposing poles of the judging process are **thinking and feeling**. We call those the judging functions. These four functions will be described later on in some detail. For the moment you simply need to understand their relationship to each other in Jung's compass.

Sensing (S)

P
E
R
C
E

Thinking (T) J U D G I N G Feeling (F)

I
V
I
N
G

iNtuition (N)

These four functions of the personality are different expressions of psychic energy or libido created by dynamic tensions between the opposing functions of the personality. In Jung's terms the libido is not limited to sexual energy. It is our God-given life energy. God loves us into life, breathing life into us. All life is Love's energy. The goal of this energy is the glory of God, which is man or woman fully alive with his or her inborn potential fully realised.

For Jung the most fundamental division of types is between the **introvert** and the **extravert**. These are opposite attitudes, focuses of attention on either the outer or the inner world. Each function at the four points of Jung's compass may operate in an extraverted way, attending to the external world of people, things and events,

or it may operate in an introverted way, attending to the internal
world of thought, reflection and ideas.

To distinguish someone's personality type, Jung said, we need
to know where that person's psychic energy is usually directed.
Some people prefer to direct it outwards (E) and others, inwards
(I). We must also discover the person's favourite way of perceiving, either sensing (S) or intuition (N), and of judging, either
thinking (T) or feeling (F).

Jung made no extreme claims for his theory. It is not meant to
give an exact picture of the workings of the human mind, or a
complete explanation of personality differences. In its elegance
and simplicity Jung's theory of psychological types reminds me of
a Metro or Underground map. Placed over a topographical map of
the city, the London Underground map is hopelessly inaccurate.
Yet for discovering where you are in relation to other underground
stations, or how best to travel from Charing Cross to London
Bridge, or from Watford to Cockfosters, the Underground map is
unsurpassed.

## The Myers-Briggs Type Indicator (MBTI™)

Jung said, in effect, 'If my theory works, use it!' And work it does,
very accurately indeed, as can be attested by the hundreds of
thousands of people who have used the Myers-Briggs Type Indicator (MBTI).

The MBTI, developed over a period of forty years by two
American women, Katharine Briggs and her daughter Isabel
Myers, is probably now the most used psychological instrument in
the world. It is not a test, with right or wrong answers and better
or worse results, but a self-report inventory of 126 forced choice
questions about our preferences and about the ways we usually
feel or act.

The MBTI points us to one of sixteen possible personality types
that is our particular colour on the rainbow of humanity. Each of
the sixteen types has its own recognisable characteristics that are a
result of our habitual patterns of behaviour and relationships.

## Be Yourself

The model of personality described by Jung and used by the MBTI speaks to Christians of the balance, harmony and perfection of the Person of God. Each human person, created in God's image and likeness, has particular gifts of personality that we must appreciate and develop.

In Romans 12 Paul encourages Christians to think of themselves with sober judgement and to recognise the many differing and complementary gifts in the body of Christ, the Church. This theme is taken up in Ephesians 4. As we learn to recognise and use our individual share of the gifts of grace, so we will grow together into Christ until we become fully mature with the fullness of Christ himself.

There is a proper fear abroad that the Myers-Briggs typology may be abused by using it to limit people, stereotype them, pigeon-hole them and label them with letters like INFJ and ESTP. Insofar as the MBTI helps you to understand a little better how you tick, and appreciate a little more your own and other people's God-given gifts of personality, it is an extremely valuable tool. The MBTI, properly used, is positive, encouraging, and powerfully liberating. For your individual journey of self-discovery, it is an accurate compass.

You have a vocation to be yourself. You are called to become you, that unique person whom God had in mind from the beginning of creation. When Rabbi Zuscha was dying he was asked what questions he thought God would put to him when he got to heaven. 'I'm not sure,' he said, 'except of one thing. God won't be saying to me, "Why weren't you Moses?", or "Why weren't you David?", but "Why weren't you Zuscha?" '

We will now take a more detailed look at the psychological attitudes and functions, and their corresponding personality traits.


## Extraversion (E) and Introversion (I)

These terms, from the vocabulary of depth psychology, are now in everyday use as descriptions of sociability. We describe a loud, talkative, friendly, gregarious person as extravert and we may call someone an introvert who is quiet, withdrawn, solitary and unsociable.

There is some truth in those distinctions but they are caricatures.

In fact, some introverts are very sociable and noisy, while some extraverts are shy, quiet people. Introverts are often good on stage, and many actors and clergy prefer the introverted attitude.

I think of two of my friends, Ann and Jim. Ann is someone who is easy to get to know while Jim is more reflective and has hidden depths. Those differences relate to the way Ann and Jim naturally and usually focus their energy.

Ann's focus tends to be extraverted, directed outwards towards the external world. The activity and relationships of the outer world energise her. If she is on her own for too long she gets tired and frazzled and has to recharge by visiting or telephoning friends.

Jim's energy, though, is introverted. His focus of attention is directed inwards to his private world of thought and ideas, and there he finds his energy. If Jim has to be giving out to others for too long, he becomes exhausted. If for a long period he is denied the opportunity for private introverted time, he becomes very irritable, even dissociated, and starts bumping into things.

Sociability is an art that anyone can learn. It is not how well you get on with other people that distinguishes these two psychological attitudes, E and I, but how you prefer to direct your psychic energy. When you are extraverting one of the four functions, S, N, T or F, the flow of energy and the focus of attention are outwards, away from yourself towards the outer world of people, events, objects and external activity. When you are introverting a function the flow of energy is in the opposite direction, from the object to the subject, so that the focus of attention is the inner world of thought, reflection, ideas and imagination.

## I Personality Traits

Introversion-preferring people (Is) work out their mental processes in the inner world. They carry on long conversations with themselves in their heads. They might say, 'I don't want to speak until I've had time to think about it'. When they do speak, what comes out is often a considered statement.

I-preferring people often enjoy extraverted activities such as working with others or going to a party but it will tire them much more than if they were E-preferring. Is need to renew their energy by introversion and therefore they need privacy to recharge. The Is' battery is recharged by taking it out of the car and connecting it to the battery charger in the garage.

## E Personality Traits

The Es' battery, on the other hand, is recharged by driving down a busy motorway in the company of hundreds of other cars. Es are energised by extraversion and need relationships and external activities to recharge.

E types often enjoy introverted activity, such as quiet, reflective time alone, but it will tire them much more than if they were I-preferring.

E-preferring people more often work out their mental processes in the outer world. They might say, 'I don't know what I think until I've said it!'

## Your Preference for E or I

Extraversion and introversion are your God-given ability to live beyond yourself in the breadth of life and live within yourself in the depth of life. We all extravert and introvert, every day. For balance and harmony in our lives we need to do both. Both ways of directing and renewing our psychic energy are good and valuable, *but one rather than the other will be your particular gift*. The important question for discovering your own personality type is, 'What is my natural, easiest and usually preferred attitude? Is it extraversion, or is it introversion?'

It may not be immediately obvious to you that you have a genuine preference for E or for I. Sometimes natural preferences are obscured by the influences of upbringing, environment, education, or the demands of work or family. Perhaps you think that you should not prefer either E or I, and that the best and most balanced place to be is on the centre point of the EI scale. That, however, is more often a place of tension than of balance.

## Sensing (S) and Intuition (N) – Perceiving Functions

The perceiving process functions in two distinct ways, either by **Sensing (S)** or by **iNtuition (N)**.

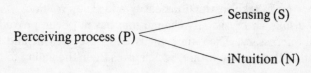

Perceiving process (P) — Sensing (S) / iNtuition (N)

Whenever we become aware of anything, our perceiving process will be taking us along either the **Sensing (S)** route or the **iNtuition (N)** route. Both routes provide good and equally valid ways of becoming aware of anything.

You are travelling along the S route whenever you pay attention to specific facts and realities, using your five senses of sight, hearing, smell, taste and touch.

You are on the N route, perceiving with your intuitive function, whenever you become aware of anything through any means other than your five senses. N perceptions come as hunches, ideas, associations, patterns and possibilities arising from the unconscious.

We all use both ways of perceiving, but from birth each of us will come to prefer one rather than the other – either the S function or the N function. That preference, and our use of it in either an extraverted way or an introverted way, will have a profound effect on our personality.

Those who naturally prefer S perception will enjoy using that route. They will give it right of way. The more they use it and become familiar with it, the faster they can travel along it. The S route becomes a highway, smooth, wide and well lit, while the less-preferred N route remains a narrow, winding lane with high hedges, full of pot-holes and hidden hazards, enjoyable but slow and tiring to drive along.

People whose natural preference for perceiving is N will habitually give intuition the right of way. For them, the N route will have been worked on and improved over the years until it is the fast track. For N-preferring people, it is their S route that becomes the narrow, winding lane with high hedges on both sides and an obstacle round every corner.

*S Personality Traits*

Ss are usually detailed, observant, practical, realistic, 'feet on the ground' people. They notice facts and trust them. Experience, for the S, is the most reliable guide for future action.

S types often take instructions easily and enjoy routines. They tend to dislike and resist any change that has not been proved to be really necessary. Their time focus is on the present and the past, rather than on the future, which gives them the ability to live in the here-and-now in a way that the more future-oriented N types often envy or admire.

Their way of perceiving moves clearly from step to step, so they are usually not satisfied that they have the correct answer unless they can see the working. 'Prove it', they will say. 'Show me!'

Extraverted Sensing types are constantly scanning the outer world in a very matter-of-fact way and picking up clear sensory impressions. Once the sensation has gone, they do not think twice about it, but move on to the next S perception, so they live constantly in the present moment. That ability can help them become very skilled performers in entertainment and sport.

Extraverted Sensing people often shop in a spontaneous, spur-of-the-moment way and they can be quite self-indulgent. You can see them scanning the displays in department stores, handling the merchandise, trying clothes on, and saying, 'I like it, so I'll buy it.'

Introverted Sensing types, on the other hand, have vivid internal sensory impressions. They select things in the outer world to take inside for their subjective impressions, and they place great value on experience. So they usually shop more carefully and less spontaneously, reading the consumer magazines, comparing, researching and marshalling all the relevant facts in their minds before buying.

Their attention tends to be much more selective than the extraverted Sensing types. They record facts and sensory details in their minds, and often can recall them with remarkable intensity and accuracy, remembering what people looked like, what they wore and what they said days, weeks or even months before.

In Myers-Briggs theory the types for whom Sensing is extraverted are ESTP, ESFP, ISTP and ISFP; and the types with introverted Sensing are ISTJ, ISFJ, ESTJ and ESFJ. However, we must remember 'each type has a number of variants caused by "non-standard" arrangements of the four functions.'[1] Many people are exceptions to the theory and do not necessarily prefer to extravert or introvert their functions as the MBTI would predict.


## N Personality Traits

People who habitually prefer the intuitive function perceive most easily and naturally through a kind of sixth sense. They rely on unconscious patterns and associations, and they have inexplicable and accurate hunches that often fascinate or infuriate S-types. Ns tend to be imaginative, inspirational and creative. They are at home with abstractions, concepts, and metaphor. Intuitive types are inventive and theoretical people, who like to imagine possibilities.

Ns see the big picture. Indeed, they can sometimes see the wood so clearly that they fail to notice the trees. They like the challenge and excitement of change and variety. They work in bursts of enthusiasm and energy.

Extraverted Intuitive types want to use their vision to change the world. They love to find new and ingenious ways of doing things. Extraverted N types will happily promote and develop other people's ideas. They are frequently sidetracked by new interesting possibilities out there in the wide world and so lose interest in a current idea or project before it is completed.

Introverted Intuitive types usually like to generate their own ideas. They are the most creative and original of all the types. Their lives are directed by inner awareness of possibilities that they want other people to put into practice.

In Myers-Briggs theory the types for whom Intuition is extraverted are ENTP, ENFP, INTP and INFP; and the types with introverted Intuition are INTJ, INFJ, ENTJ, ENFJ. However, we must remember that many people are exceptions to the theory and do not necessarily prefer to extravert or introvert their functions in the order that the MBTI would predict.

Ss and Ns often misunderstand each other because they see things in different ways. However, they are complementary types. They need each other. The N is the visionary, the thinker-upper, who can spark off new ideas and come up with ingenious solutions to problems. The S is the realist, the doer, who can check the facts and patiently attend to the detailed and routine work required to put the Ns' ideas into action.

## Your Preference for S or N

If you want to do a little exercise that might help you discover your own preference for S or N, write down a few sentences about a rose – before reading the next paragraph.

You can often detect whether what has been written comes from sensing perceptions or from intuitive perceptions. Sometimes it is a description, with a precise, factual, S feel about it. For instance, a Sensing-preferring person might write something like this: 'A rose is a flower often grown in gardens, as bushes or as standard roses. There are many colours and varieties of roses. The old-fashioned ones often have a strong scent.'

An iNtuition-preferring person is likely to dwell on the association and memories sparked off by the thought of a rose, and that will give their sentences an intuitive ring. For example, 'A red rose is the flower of love. It is its beauty which matters, not its name. That which we call a rose, by any other name would smell as sweet.' One man in a workshop got carried away by this exercise, saying that a rose reminded him of confidentiality. Eventually we traced that thought back to the phrase *sub rosa*, from the use of the rose as a symbol of silence placed over confessionals in the sixteenth century. That is a typical example of the way Ns leap about in their perceptive process, and have to work their way back to explain where their ideas came from.

## Thinking (T) and Feeling (F) – Judging Functions

The judging process also functions in two distinct ways, either by **Thinking (T)** or by **Feeling (F)**.

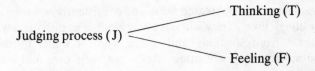

Judging process (J)
Thinking (T)
Feeling (F)

Whenever we do anything with the data that comes to us through our perceptions (that is, through S or N), our judging process will take us along either the **Thinking (T)** route or the **Feeling (F)** route. Both routes provide good and equally valid ways of handling our perceptions by reaching conclusions, forming opinions and making decisions.

You are travelling along the **T** route whenever you handle your S or N perceptions in an objective, logical and analytical way – when you stand back and ask, 'Is this decision right, or is it wrong?'

You are on the **F** route, using your feeling function, whenever you make a judgement based on your personal, subjective values. F-preferring people will characteristically ask, 'How do I feel about that? Is it a good decision or a bad one?'

We all use both ways of judging. We can never use both functions at the same time, just as you can never be travelling east and west at the same time, but we can swop from one to another in a split second. Each of us will have an inborn preference for either the T function or the F function. That preference, combined with our preferred perceiving function, S or N, will greatly affect our personality.

Some people will habitually give T judgement the right of way. T will be their fast track and, for them, the F route will be slow, tiring and full of possible pitfalls. Other people by nature and habit will give right of way to F judgement, and will be less skilful and confident when going down the T route.

## T Personality Traits

T-preferring people look for consistency and objective accuracy. They characteristically ask, 'Is that true or false?' They are objective and see things clearly from the outside looking in; and so they tend to be good at impersonal, critical analysis. They also take criticism well, as a helpful way of discovering truth.

Ts are often clear and concise communicators. They can generally stand up to opposition, holding fast to the objective principles in any situation. Ts often have a passionate concern for justice. They want people to be treated fairly and consistently and they are good at 'tough love'. They will not allow conflict or disharmony to deter them from speaking and doing what is right. In their decision-making they will often screen out their own and other people's emotions.

People who extravert their Thinking function want to use their objective rationality to control and change the world. They are often organisers and managers who want to get involved in the problems around them, find solutions, and get things done.

Those who introvert their Thinking function are more interested in thinking deeply about problems. Introverted Ts are often so absorbed with their own mental processes that they are oblivious to what is going on around them. They want to analyse and understand situations and get to the bottom of things. They offer insight and expertise. In contrast to the extraverted Ts, their concern is not so much with changing the world as with changing people's minds and their way of understanding.

In Myers-Briggs theory the types for whom Thinking is extraverted are ESTJ, ENTJ, ISTJ and INTJ; and the types with introverted Thinking are ISTP, INTP, ESTP, ENTP. However, we must remember that many people are exceptions to the theory and do not necessarily prefer to extravert or introvert their functions as the MBTI would predict.

It would be a mistake to think that T types lack what is usually thought of as feeling. 'Thinking' and 'Feeling' are used by Jung in a specialised way to refer to particular types of mental functions. So we must always remember that Thinking types 'feel', just as Feeling types 'think'. Ts are often passionate about their ideas, and Fs often think deeply about their feelings. Nevertheless, Ts generally want to *understand* emotions, whereas Fs are more interested in *experiencing* emotions.

## F Personality Traits

F types are 'people people', empathic, tactful, encouraging and appreciative. They decide with the heart rather than the head. They tend to take things to heart and can be greatly hurt by crticism, which they usually take very personally.

Fs are subjective. In a group, they are not objective observers like the Ts, but they see everything from the point of view of the participants. Their great concern is for harmony, external harmonious relationships for the extraverted Fs and inner harmony for the introverted Fs. Extraverted Fs are much more expressive about themselves and others than people whose Feeling is introverted. Introverted Fs have intense and deep commitments and loyalties that may not be readily observable or outwardly expressed.

Conflict for Fs can be very stressful. For extraverted Fs that conflict is likely to come about when their values and ideals do not match up with external situations, the community, society and the world. Introverted Feeling types are usually more committed to protecting and promoting their ideals and loyalties and anything that puts those under threat will create stress, which they may well internalise.

An example of the way in which the threatened introverted F can operate was related to me by a colleague. A priest became very hurt and upset during a meeting of clergy. If he had been an extraverted F type he would have voiced his distress but this man appeared impassive and said nothing. However, after the meeting he went home and vented his deeply wounded F values by writing an angry letter to all his colleagues.

Fs often have more difficulty than Ts where hard decisions have to be taken concerning people. They may want to draw attention to mitigating circumstances. However, it is important to remember that F judgement is rational and not (as some Ts may claim) driven by emotion. The well-developed F function shows itself in a mature and strong system of personal values that are the touchstone for all their decisions.

In Myers-Briggs theory the types for whom Feeling is extraverted are ESFJ, ENFJ, ISFJ and INFJ; and the types with introverted Feeling are ISFP, INFP, ESFP and ENFP. However, we must remember that many people are exceptions to the theory and do not necessarily prefer to extravert or introvert their functions as the MBTI would predict.

When Ts and Fs do not value each other's differing gifts, they can misunderstand each other and clash, the Fs seeing the Ts as cold and heartless, and the Ts dismissing the Fs as fickle and woolly-minded. In fact, of course, each needs the other, and we need both within ourselves. The F needs the T to uphold firm impersonal principles, to insist on nothing less than the truth and to analyse the evidence. The T needs the F to be tactful, to explain how others will feel, to conciliate, persuade and appreciate.

## Your Preference for T or F

If you do not already know your preference for T or F, you may be able to detect it by writing down some thoughts about love, and then reading the following paragraphs.

Fs tend to begin with the experience and then move on to definition. They will give examples of what love means to them, how it is expressed, and how all-embracing it is – the most wonderful thing in the world!

Ts will often find a word like 'love' difficult to get to grips with. It is too slippery and subjective for them. They will want to say, 'What sort of love do you mean?' Unlike the Fs, the Ts will often begin by trying to define the various kinds of love. They will want to point out that love involves the will, and is much more than an emotional feeling.

## Perceiving (P) or Judging (J) − The Preferred Process

This feature of personality type is an attitude, an observable life-style, which is implicit in Jung's theory and drawn out by Myers and Briggs. It is a preference for one or other of the arms of the compass. Each of us, in our outer lifestyle, prefers either the **Perceiving process (P)** or the **Judging process (J)**.

Be careful to note that regardless of our preference for extraversion or introversion, this J or P preference refers to the way we like to behave in the *outer world*. Everyone has a lifestyle that betrays a natural preference for either the perceiving process or the judging process. Given the choice, would you rather take in information (P) or deal with information (J)?

Those who prefer P will live their outer lives with their preferred perceiving function, which will be either S or N. Those who prefer J like to live their outer lives with their preferred judging function, either T or F.

## J Personality Traits

J-preferring people tend to live their lives in a decisive, structured and planned way. They like to control life and have things organised. Even if their homes, kitchens, or desks look untidy and disorganised, they know where everything is and what has to be done and woe betide anyone who tidies up their chaos!

Js will often have a strong work-ethic. They are much more likely than Ps to overwork and to feel guilty about taking time off. They are generally good at keeping deadlines and often like to make lists of priorities and tick them off, with a feeling of satisfaction, as they are completed.

They like to come to closure; they like making decisions. If there is a decision around waiting to be made, a J-preferring person will feel tense and uncomfortable and cannot relax until that decision has been made.

## P Personality Traits

A J friend tells me that she hates going shopping with her P husband, simply because he takes so long to make up his mind. 'He goes out to buy a new pair of trousers, finds exactly what he is looking for in the first shop he goes to, but then he feels compelled to spend hours trying on trousers in every other men's outfitter in town before finally ending up buying a new pair of slippers instead. It sends me mad!'

Ps may feel tense and uncomfortable when there is a decision to be made and there is not, in their opinion, sufficient information available to make it. When Ps do make a decision, they are more likely than Js to think of it as provisional rather than final.

As Perceivers, they are natural collectors of information. They too make lists, but they are lists of things they might like to do some time, maybe, when they get round to it. Js use lists, Ps lose them. A deadline, for a P, is a signal to start work. They are not particularly prone to guilty feelings about taking time off, even if their work is not finished. Ps want to enjoy life rather than control it, and so their lifestyle tends to be open, relaxed, spontaneous and flexible.

Again, there is a danger that we will misunderstand and conflict with those who have the opposite preference to our own. Ps can see Js as rigid, demanding and workaholics. Js can see Ps as disorganised, fickle and irresponsible. However, Js can be very open to information and when necessary Ps can be very decisive. As with all the pairs of preferences, they complement one another. The J needs the P to avoid making hasty and ill-informed decisions and to see that life is there to be enjoyed. The J can help the P to make necessary decisions, to fulfil work responsibilities and meet deadlines.

Each of us uses both attitudes but the P or J in our type description will always refer to the attitude we prefer in our extraverted lives.

J types are organised and decisive in their extraverted lives, which they live with their judging function (T or F). However, inwardly, in their introverted lives, their opposite perceiving function (S or N) holds sway, giving a complementarity and balance to the personality. In their inner world, Js will often surprise themselves by being very open, receptive and flexible.

Similarly, P types like to 'go with the flow' in their extraverted lives, which they live with their perceiving function (S or N). However, inwardly, in their introverted lives, they are much more planned, organised and clear about their goals. The introverted life of a P type is run by the J function (T or F), giving balance to the personality.

## Your Preference for P or J

Do you have a feeling of restlessness and urgency when there is a decision around, waiting to be made? And then, when the decision has been made, a feeling of relief? If so, you are probably a J-preferring person.

Or do you want to leave things open, and feel a resistance about making a decision? And afterwards, when the decision has been made, do you feel uncomfortable about it, and want to remake it? If so, your preference is probably for P.

# 3

# The Dynamics of Type

We have seen that the MBTI uses just four basic psychological dimensions:

1. In which direction does my energy prefer to flow? These are called the Attitudes of:

   | **Extraversion (E)** | or | **Introversion (I)** |
   |---|---|---|
   | The outer world of people, things and external activity | | The inner world of ideas, and the activity of reflection and thought |

2. How do I prefer to become aware of anything? These are called the Perceiving Functions of:

   | **Sensing (S)** | or | **iNtuition (N)** |
   |---|---|---|
   | Becoming aware through the five senses | | Becoming aware in an intuitive way through patterns and associations |

3. How do I prefer to make decisions and form opinions? These are called the Judging Functions of:

   | **Thinking (T)** | or | **Feeling (F)** |
   |---|---|---|
   | Objective, logical, 'true or false' | | Subjective, personal, 'good or bad' |

4. Do I prefer to use a Judging Function or a Perceiving Function in my external life? These are called the Attitudes of:

   | **Judging (J)** | or | **Perceiving (P)** |
   |---|---|---|
   | Decisive, structured, controls life | | Open, flexible, curious, adapts to life |

## Preferences

From birth, each of us comes to prefer one from each of those four pairs. Your particular preferences, for E or I, S or N, T or F, J or P, will indicate your personality type. The possible combinations give the sixteen Myers-Briggs types:

| ISTJ | ISFJ | INFJ | INTJ |
|------|------|------|------|
| ISTP | ISFP | INFP | INTP |
| ESTP | ESFP | ENFP | ENTP |
| ESTJ | ESFJ | ENFJ | ENTJ |

To discover your type, with or without the help of the MBTI, you must learn to detect your own habitual preferences, and that is not always easy. You might like to try this simple experiment:

1. Take a pen and paper and sign your name.
2. Now put the pen in your other hand (your less-preferred hand) and sign your name again. Then copy out a sentence or two from this page, still writing with your less-preferred hand.
3. Now jot down a list of words that describe *what it felt like* when you were writing with your less-preferred hand.

The first thing to learn from this experiment is that your psychological preferences are so ingrained that you hardly ever think about them. You take them for granted. When you signed your name you naturally took the pen in the hand you normally use for writing. You did not think, 'Which hand shall I write with today?' You simply picked up the pen and wrote with your preferred hand, the right one if you are right-handed and the left if you are left-handed.

In the same way as you reached for the pen with your preferred hand, you habitually turn to your preferred attitudes and functions. You spontaneously move towards either Introversion or Extraversion to focus your life energy and recharge your batteries. To become aware of the existence of anything you will habitually and unthinkingly use one perceiving function, Sensing or iNtuition, rather than the other. When you make a decision or form an opinion, you will naturally and unintentionally turn to your preferred judging function, either Thinking or Feeling. In your outer lifestyle, you will naturally incline towards the decisive Judging attitude or the receptive Perceiving attitude.

It is not easy to know yourself. Your habitual psychological preferences come into play so easily that most of the time you are not even aware of them. They are so ingrained in you that you take them for granted. They are so natural that you can easily imagine that everyone shares, or ought to share, your own particular preferences.

You may see your own preferences clearly or you may rather confusingly see all the preferences at work in yourself and find it hard to believe that you favour one way of seeing things, or of deciding things, over the other. Your habitual, ingrained preferences may not be at all clear to you, though others can sometimes see them more clearly.

The 'handedness' experiment may also remind you not to attach value judgements to psychological preferences. Most people are right-handed, some are left-handed. In a world full of things designed for right-handed people there are some disadvantages for those who are left-handed, but to say that it is wrong to be left-handed, or that they could be genuinely right-handed if they tried, is absurd. Even if they have been forced or trained to go against their natural preference, that does not alter how they really are. The fact remains that each individual is born with one preference rather than the other, to be either right-handed or left-handed.

It is exactly the same with your innate psychological preferences. It is not better or worse, right or wrong, to be an intuitive-preferring person rather than a sensing-preferring person, or someone who prefers extraversion rather than introversion. However, you must be on your guard because you can be very biased and arrogant about your own preferences. If you are in the majority, as for instance Es are, the minority who are introverts can be made to feel handicapped, inadequate, or wrong.

For example, an introverted child in a family where everyone else is an extravert may well grow up with the idea that extraversion is natural and right and introversion is unnatural and wrong. A colleague told me this story about her own experience as an introverted child.

When I was a little girl I used to love going to my bedroom and spending hours on my own, reading and playing games with imaginary playmates. The other members of my family were all extraverts. Whenever I came downstairs to rejoin them after spending some time on my own, my mother would say, in a very kind and concerned way, 'Are you all right, dear?' I got the impression that somehow I shouldn't be all right, that wanting to be alone was abnormal. Since those childhood days I have thought it wrong to be an introvert. I've tried very hard to be an extravert but it's an exhausting effort for me. Now that I've become aware of my genuine preference for introversion, and know that it's not wrong, I feel freed from a great burden. I still feel guilty about being an introvert – those tapes still play in my mind, but they play quieter, and I can now choose to ignore the false guilt. Awareness of my personality type has freed me to be myself, as God has made me, without feeling that I am somehow deficient as a person.

The 'exhausting effort' of using functions and attitudes that are not your true preference is illustrated by the last part of the 'handedness' experiment, when you considered how it felt to write with your less-preferred hand. You probably jotted down words like slow, clumsy, shaky, uncontrolled, challenging, interesting, annoying, fun. Writing with the other hand takes concentration and conscious effort and the result often looks childish and immature. So, too, your less-preferred and therefore less-used functions and attitudes remain relatively undeveloped and so are more tiring and much slower routes for acquiring and handling information.

You need and use both your hands. Indeed, for some activities, such as playing the harp, the skilful use of both hands is essential. Similarly, each of us has access to all four attitudes (E and I, J and P) and all four mental functions (S and N, T and F). You prefer one of each pair, but that does not imply that you do not have or need or use the others.

## Your Personality Type

The best way to begin to get to know your own personality type is to complete the MBTI and have it scored and interpreted to you by a qualified practitioner. If you can take part in a Myers-Briggs workshop, you will have the added advantage of being able to discuss and verify your type with other people of other types.

The four letters reported to you by the Indicator are a good working hypothesis, nothing more. Some, probably most, people are comfortable with their indicated type and as time goes on are increasingly convinced of its accuracy. Others are uncertain about one or more of the indicated preferences and it could take years for them to grow into a confident knowledge and acceptance of their true type.

There are two points to be noted here. The first is that the MBTI merely reflects back the answers you have given to its 126 forced-choice questions. Those answers may have been influenced by many factors other than your natural and genuine preferences, such as the pressures on you of work, family or church. The practitioner will not and cannot 'tell you' what your type is.

The second point is that the MBTI is an affirming instrument. It has nothing to do with stereotyping, labelling, or boxing people in; on the contrary, it helps us know ourselves and others in a new way. Knowledge of type releases us to be ourselves, to gain new insight, and to rejoice in the special gifts of personality with which God has endowed us.

Much misrepresentation and misunderstanding of the Myers-Briggs typology comes about because the dynamics of type are not thoroughly understood and appreciated. The functions and attitudes are presented as if they existed in isolation from one another – 'as if the MBTI merely reported preferences on four separate scales. For instance, an ESFP type is misleadingly caricatured as someone who has Extraversion plus Sensing plus Feeling plus Perceiving, and who is deficient in Introversion, iNtuition, Thinking and Judging.

If you try to use all four functions equally, they will all remain slow and difficult routes. None will have right of way over the others. In psychological terms, none of the functions will be well differentiated in your consciousness. Growth comes not so much by trying hard to use all four functions equally well, as by recognising your individual gifts of personality and then learning to use those gifts well.

In Romans 12 St Paul urges each of his readers to judge one's self soberly, in the light of his or her differing gifts. That good advice can be applied to all God's gifts of grace, including your individual gifts of personality. It is vitally important to focus on your strengths and use them as good stewards of your life. Then, and only then, will you be able to bring the weaker parts of your character into consciousness so that the light of Christ can shine on them too, to reflect in you more and more of God's glory.

Remember, then, that you have all the psychological functions and attitudes common to humanity. You have all four attitudes, E and I, J and P, and all four mental functions, S and N, T and F. They relate dynamically to one another, outwardly and inwardly, in an astonishingly subtle way. That dynamic relationship influences not only the surface traits of your personality but also your habits of mind and behaviour, your interests, needs and values, your relationships, and in particular your prayer-relationship with God.

## Type and Taste

You may be thinking, 'How in the world can four mental functions have any profound bearing on my personality, which I know is so mysterious and complex?' I find it helpful to think of this question in relation to taste and colour.

Imagine these different tastes:

> vanilla ice-cream
> cucumber sandwiches
> Christmas pudding
> vegetable curry
> syrup of figs
> fresh crusty bread
> gooseberries
> buttered parsnips

The range and variety of tastes are vast. Even within one particular type of food, such as cheese, there are dozens of distinctive tastes – Stilton, Edam, Camembert, Lancashire, Parmesan, to name but a few. Or consider the multitude of types of wines in the world, each with its distinctive flavour and character.

The surprising fact is that all the subtleties of taste and flavour are appreciated by us through a combination of just *four* kinds of taste. Our taste buds recognise only sweet, sour, salty and bitter. The vast range of tastes can be traced back to four basic qualities, just as each one of the immense variety of personality types is a dynamic and developing interaction of just four mental functions, Sensing, iNtuition, Thinking and Feeling.

## The Dominant and Auxiliary Functions

You all use all the four functions, but you do not use them equally well. Think of them as languages, and you can say that everyone speaks S and N and T and F. One of those four will be your mother tongue, the language you speak most naturally and fluently and the least self-consciously. You have grown up to express yourself with it and you use it, probably very skilfully, without having to think about it. That mother-tongue of your personality, whether it is sensing, intuition, thinking or feeling, is called your **dominant** function.

If you are an E, an extraverting-preferring person, that favourite dominant function of yours will be extraverted. In other words, you will use it to relate to the outer world of people and things. On the other hand, if you are an I, an introverting-preferring person, that favourite dominant function of yours will be introverted. You will use it to relate to your inner world of thought and reflection. There is a golden rule here, which is that you always use your favourite function in your favourite world.

Your second-best language will not be quite as fluent but by the time you are adult you will probably have learned to read and speak it very well. It supports and supplements your dominant and is called your **auxiliary** function.

## Balance and Complementarity

The dominant and auxiliary functions, indicated in the middle letters of your Myers-Briggs type, complement each other. So if your dominant is one of the two perceiving functions (S or N) your auxiliary will be one of the two judging functions (T or F). By the same token, if your dominant is a judging function, your auxiliary will be a perceiving function. In this way the dominant and auxiliary functions provide an essential balance in each personality between the perceiving process, which is passive and receptive, and the judging process, which is active and decisive. As we will see, your prayer should reflect that balance.

Extraverts relate to the outer world with their favourite function, their dominant, and they introvert with their auxiliary function. It follows that an extravert's auxiliary function will not be as visible as the dominant, but it will be used to relate to the inner world of ideas and reflection.

Introverts use their dominant function to relate to their inner world, and use their second-best auxiliary function for extraverting. That is why introverts are very often undervalued by people who do not know them well. It takes time to discover their hidden qualities. Unlike extraverts, who show their best to the world, introverts reserve their best for their inner life and reveal to the world their second-best. The dominant function of introverts is invisible. When people do glimpse it, you will hear such comments as, 'I never knew he had that in him!', 'She has hidden depths!', 'He's a dark horse!'

So we must beware of making snap judgements about people, especially about introverts. And those of us who are introverts must come to recognise that our most precious gift of personality lies within. It may not be how people see us, unless they know us really well; and it may not be what other people have told us about our personalities.

## How to Discover the Dominant and Auxiliary

You will remember that the J and P attitudes point to our preferred lifestyle *in the outer world*.

J types use their judging function, T or F, in the outer, extraverted world.

If they are E– –J types, then that T or F function will be their dominant. It is their favourite function that they use in their favourite world. The perceiving function, S or N, will be their auxiliary. If, however, they are I– –J types, their favourite world is the inner one, and so the extraverted T or F function will be for them their second-best, their auxiliary. The dominant for them will be the function they use in their favourite introverted world, the perceiving S or N function.

P types use their perceiving function, S or N, in the outer, extraverted world. If they are E– –P types, then that S or N function will be their dominant, and their judging function, T or F, will be their auxiliary. If, however, they are I– –P types, the extraverted S or N function will be their auxiliary, and their dominant will be the judging T or F function.

## The Tertiary and Inferior Functions

Your third 'language' is one which you would not usually speak out of choice. You can communicate in it when you have to, but your accent is bad, your vocabulary is limited, and you often make grammatical mistakes. However, in business and pleasure it is often a useful and enjoyable language to have at your command. It is the **tertiary** function, always the opposite of your auxiliary function. If your auxiliary is N your tertiary is S, if your auxiliary is T your tertiary is F, and so on.

The fourth 'language', your least reliable and least used, is of particular interest in thinking about your prayer-relationship with God.

Usually you can just about get by in that fourth language. You can order a cup of coffee, ask directions, and make polite and stilted conversation. But your grasp of that least favourite language is so slight that you are slow and clumsy with it. Speaking it takes effort and you make many mistakes. People laugh at you or get exasperated with you, making you feel awkward and embarrassed. By mid-life, however, that fourth language begins to come into its own. You discover to your delight that it opens up new frontiers for you, new pleasures, new possibilities in life, new relationships. Nevertheless, it always remains inferior, and it is usually known as the **inferior** function. You can easily identify it in your type, because it is always the one that is at the opposite pole of your dominant, and it also usually has the opposite attitude (E or I) to the dominant. Every strength carries with it a corresponding weakness, and the weakest, inferior function is the opposite to your strongest, most preferred, dominant function.

## The Development of the Functions

When you were a baby the four functions of your personality were undifferentiated. As you grew and your personality developed, so the two pairs of functions, S and N, T and F, gradually became untangled. One of the four moved into consciousness as the dominant function and its opposite dropped into the unconscious as the weakest, inferior function. From the other pair, one tended towards consciousness as the auxiliary function in the service of your dominant, and its opposite became your tertiary function, unconscious but more accessible than your inferior function.

As a grown person, all four functions are at your disposal to use appropriately, though you will never be able to use them equally well. You have within yourself opposite needs and instincts, and the tension between them gives you your vigour and zest for life.

Your inferior function, however, never ceases to be inferior. It is childish, touchy, and troublesome. Nevertheless, when you do recognise it you discover in yourself a rich source of tremendous enjoyment and energy. Jung thought of the inferior function as a friend and guide. Properly valued, it will lead you to new avenues of prayer.

## The Troublesome Inferior

From time to time you find yourself saying, 'I don't know what came over me', 'I don't know why I had that horrible thought', 'I wish I hadn't said that', or 'I wasn't being myself just then'. When that happens, the chances are that you are talking about your inferior function.

This happens for a variety of reasons. When you are tired, ill, overstressed, or under the influence of alcohol, the usual restraints of your personality are weakened. You are off balance. If you have ever tried to sit on a beach ball in a swimming pool, you will know that it takes some pressure to keep the ball under and when you lose your balance it bursts up to the surface. In the same kind of way, when you are psychologically off balance, the inferior function may surface into consciousness with alarming force.

Sometimes an emotionally charged situation may hook your inferior function out of your unconscious. Before you know where you are, it is there in your conscious, causing you trouble.

Over-playing your dominant function at the expense of the other three may also cause your inferior function to emerge, to restore the balance and harmony of your psyche.

The inferior, and in some cases the tertiary, function lives in the unconscious personality, sometimes called the Shadow. When it emerges, it brings up from the depths 'not merely incompatible and rejected remnants of everyday life, or inconvenient and objectionable animal tendencies, but also germs of new life and vital possibilities for the future.'[1] It is through play, recreation, hobbies and through prayer that you meet your inferior function as a friend and guide.

## Inferior Sensing

Dominant iNtuitive types (INFJ, INTJ, ENFP, ENTP) have Sensing as their inferior function.

When their inferior sensing flips unbidden into consciousness, it often appears in the form of compulsive pleasure-seeking, overeating, and accident-prone behaviour. Under stress, dominant Ns can become obsessively detailed, disturbed by small particulars which usually they would not even notice. Gripped by inferior sensing, Ns may uncharacteristically say things like 'I can't live in this mess'. They feel impelled to tidy up their normally chaotic home or desk and get things in order. Inferior sensing can also manifest itself in sensual ways, which may be extraverted (e.g. overeating) or introverted (e.g. sexual fantasies).

## Inferior Intuition

Dominant Sensing types (ISTJ, ISFJ, ESTP, ESFP) have iNtuition as their inferior function.

When they are tired, overstressed, and their senses are overloaded, their dominant sensing function capsizes into the unconscious and negative intuition flips to the surface, often in the form of wild hunches or unrealistic predictions. They can become depressive and obsessed with doom and gloom. Every cloud is a rain cloud; the tunnel has no light at the end of it. 'Oh, it's not worth trying', they say. 'It will never work!'

## Inferior Thinking

People whose type indicates dominant Feeling (ISFP, INFP, ESFJ, ENFJ) have Thinking as their inferior function.

People who are strong Fs by nature – warm, friendly, sympathetic, tactful – will flip into a clumsy and childish inferior Thinking when they are off balance. That often appears as obsessive, circular thinking, brooding about things. They can become huffy, distant, hypercritical, and sometimes ruthless and intentionally hurtful. Fs hooked by inferior T can become very argumentative. They have a compulsive, childish need to prove that they are right. They can also feel worthless. Dominant Fs working in caring professions, who allow their Feeling function to be overplayed, can suddenly become cold, withdrawn, and will say 'I don't care any more', 'I never want to hear another person's problems again.'

## Inferior Feeling

Dominant Thinking types (ISTP, INTP, ESTJ, ENTJ) have Feeling as their inferior function.

When inferior F erupts in a dominant Thinking type it comes up in an emotional way. Moodiness, disproportion and touchiness are always characteristic of the inferior function in its negative, out-of-control form, but no more so than in the Thinking type hooked by inferior Feeling. That inferior F may be projected, so that the T type will say to someone else, 'You are getting emotional!', or 'You need a holiday!' It may take the form of violent and irrational dislikes or infatuations. Caught by the inferior F, a dominant T who is normally so rational, calm and objective, can suddenly become over-sensitive and take things too personally. They can become obsessively over-anxious about other people's feelings, depressed and weepy.

## Playing and Praying in the Inferior

If you know what your inferior function is, you will probably recognise how it erupts when you are tired or angry. You will also know that the easiest and most natural way for you to play, by which I mean anything that you enjoy doing and refreshes you, is in your inferior function.

Prayer, like all relationships, will be easiest and most natural for you in your dominant function. However, especially in mid-life and onwards, you experience a need to move into new and less familiar and maybe less easy ways of praying.

By using the inferior function in prayer, God can come to us in new ways and with the least resistance because there we are at our weakest. Where we are strong we can say in effect to God, 'I'm managing OK, Lord – but if I need any help I'll let you know'. Your inferior function is the weak spot, your Achilles Heel, the vulnerable point in you where God can pierce the depth of your being with his reality (S), vision (N), love (F) and truth (T).

When this happens, your relationship with God becomes more integrated and touches every part of your being, including the hidden levels of the unconscious. That Shadow part of yourself, of which the inferior function is a key, then becomes the area of conversion and radical renewal in your spiritual life.

# 4

# Prayer and the Shadow

When you pray in the Shadow you are aware of God meeting you in the hidden, unconscious parts of yourself, and you bring those hidden parts to the light of God's grace. Your inferior and tertiary functions are helpful to you here, because they live most of the time in your Shadow and can help you bring it to light.

Your relationship of prayer is between God and the whole of yourself. 'And here we offer and present unto thee, O Lord, ourselves, our souls and bodies, to be a reasonable, holy and lively sacrifice unto thee.'[1] If we allow ourselves to think of prayer as anything less than that, we are in danger of trivialising it into conventional routine or a polite nod to God when we happen to notice him.

Your whole self, 'soul and body', is much more than your conscious self, your ego. The first commandment is, 'You shall love the Lord your God with all your heart, and with all your soul, and with all your mind and with all your strength'. In other words, you are to love God with the whole self, not just a spiritual part, or even a conscious part. Most of yourself is hidden from your consciousness.

Unlike the ego-centred self, the Self is the indwelling Christ, hallowing and transforming your life. In Thomas Merton's words, the Self is 'not its own center and does not orbit around itself; it is centered on God, the one center of all, which is "everywhere and nowhere," in whom all are encountered, from whom all proceed.'[2] In other words, there is nothing self-centred or egotistical about it. Preoccupation with your own little ego is morbid, hinders your relationship with others, and blunts your ability to live your life for others. It is precisely the opposite effect of Self-fulfilment, which brings to birth, in Jung's words, a 'new consciousness of human community precisely because it makes us aware of the unconscious, which unites and is common to all mankind.'[3]

## The Shadow

Much of the Shadow, particularly the personal Shadow, is made up of everything you have repressed for the sake of all that you want to be, the ideals and the standards that you have learned and accepted from your parents, friends, church, school and culture. Anything that does not fit with those standards and ideals is shoved down into the cellar of your personality where it is out of sight and, you hope, out of mind.

However, you cannot get rid of unacceptable parts of yourself as easily as that. They refuse to keep quiet. Like unruly children who have been shut out of the living room, they may not be seen but they are certainly heard. When you least expect it they suddenly erupt into your conscious life with unrestrained energy and often regrettable results. It seems to be a law of human nature that the more strongly you shut out and deny anything that does not fit your ego-ideal, the darker and more energised your Shadow becomes. 'Everyone carries a shadow', wrote Jung, 'and the less it is embodied in the individual's conscious life, the blacker and denser it is.'[4]

Your Shadow causes you trouble because it is immature, childish and unpredictable. But it is not wholly bad.[5] If one part of growing into that special person God had in mind at your making is the awareness and appreciation of your particular gifts of personality, another part is recognising and valuing the Shadow parts of you that are not as strong. There, in your weakness, you can come to God with childlike trust, relying on his strength. Nevertheless, it takes enormous effort and moral courage to face your own Shadow.

St Paul knew about the Shadow side of his personality. 'I cannot understand my own behaviour', he lamented. 'I fail to carry out the things I want to do, and I find myself doing the very things I hate.'[6] He could not avoid the Shadow any more than we can. All your efforts to ignore, stifle, subdue or censor it are worse than useless. The more you try to fight it, the more powerful and frightening it appears and the greater the power it exercises over you. Jung once said that to deal with the Shadow by trying to suppress it was just about as good as beheading would be for a headache. Your Shadow is a vital part of you that you can never destroy without losing your life. Without a Shadow, you would be insubstantial, invisible.

## The Unconscious and the Shadow Personality

Jung had a 'three-decker' model of the psyche in which consciousness is merely the thinnest upper layer. Below consciousness is the
rather thicker and less fragile realm of your unconscious Shadow
personality. That realm is called the Personal Unconscious. Below
that is the largest, deepest and most inaccessible area of the
psyche, known as the Collective Unconscious.

The Personal Unconscious contains everything that has ever
happened to you personally, everything that has at one time been
in your consciousness but is now forgotten or repressed, all the
hidden parts of yourself that are, in Jung's words, 'not yet ripe for
consciousness'.[7] Especially from mid-life onwards, the contents of
your Shadow personality become gradually 'ripe for consciousness'
and are brought into the light.

The deep-rooted level of the Collective Unconscious relates you
to the whole of humanity. From the Collective Unconscious come
the archetypes, those fundamental and primordial images and patterns that appear in the various symbols and myths of every culture
and in every age.

Jung offers us a helpful way of picturing the psyche. Think of a
vast ocean, representing the Collective and Personal Unconscious,
in which our conscious lives are tiny islands. 'Individual consciousness is based on and surrounded by an indefinitely extended unconscious psyche', which

> reaches so far beyond the boundaries of consciousness that the
> latter could easily be compared to an island in the ocean.
> Whereas the island is small and narrow, the ocean is immensely
> wide and deep and contains a life infinitely surpassing, in kind
> and degree, anything known on the island. . . Ultimately every
> individual life is at the same time the eternal life of the species.[8]

The unconscious unites humanity. Or, as John Donne put it, 'no
man is an island, entire of itself.'[9]

## Unconscious Prayer

Prayer wells up out of your unconscious, hidden self where the
Spirit dwells and works in you. Your relationship with God is
largely unconscious, in the depths where the Spirit comes to help
you in your weakness. 'For when we cannot choose words in order

to pray properly [that is, consciously], the Spirit himself expresses
our plea in a way that could never be put into words, and God
who knows everything in our hearts knows perfectly well what he
means'.[10] The unconscious depth of our being is often described in
the Bible as the 'heart'. So, for instance, in the first letter of Peter
it is not the outward show but the 'hidden self of the heart' that is
precious in the sight of God.[11] The heart, that mysterious centre of
your personality, is where God turns to you and where you are
converted to God.

The heart is also the hidden, Shadow side, where your treasure
is, the inner person which must be brought to the light and redeeming love of Christ. 'For it is from within, from men's hearts, that
evil intentions emerge: fornication, theft, murder, adultery, avar-
ice, malice, deceit, indecency, envy, slander, pride, folly.'[12]

The unconscious is the source of all that emerges into consciousness. Consciousness, in Jung's words, 'wells up from unknown
depths. In childhood it awakens gradually, and all through life it
wakes each morning out of the depths of sleep from an unconscious
condition. It is like a child that is born daily out of the primordial
womb of the unconscious.'[13]

Deep down in the roots of our unconscious is the well of life,
from which flows all that is good and beautiful – all love, all art, all
literature, all music, all true worship. 'Urgrund' is the word the
Germans use for those profound depths, which you can be aware
of only indirectly, where God is at work in you. The happy person
'is like a tree that is planted by water streams', drawing up life-
giving sustenance from hidden depths, tapping the source of
energy to grow and mature, so 'yielding its fruit in season.'[14]

That symbol of water is used in John's Gospel for the endless
potential offered by God, through Christ, in the unconscious
depths of our being. 'Whoever drinks this water', Jesus said to the
Samaritan woman at the well, 'will get thirsty again; but anyone
who drinks the water that I shall give will never be thirsty again:
the water that I shall give will turn into a spring inside him, welling
up to eternal life.'[15] All Christian spirituality points to that proges-
sion of life-giving energy, coming from deep within you and over-
flowing into consciousness.

## Dreams

Dreams are the symbolic language of the unconscious. When you learn to pay attention to your dreams, writing them down as soon as you awake and then making an effort to discover their significance, you quickly become aware of their importance for understanding the enormous wealth and energy of your unconscious life. 'A dream is a theatre in which the dreamer is himself the scene, the player, the prompter, the author, the public, and the critic.'[16] Some dreams are more important than others, impressing themselves on you in a strange and perhaps frightening way, or recurring night after night. Sometimes, with Job, you are scared with dreams and terrified with visions of the night. Even so, perhaps especially so, they are urging you to pay attention to whatever it is that the wisdom of your unconscious is trying to express to your conscious mind.

The unconscious will often use your dreams to urge you to face up to faults that you have tried to hide from yourself, your secret sins, your unacknowledged fears and fantasies. Your dreams may also point to those things that have got out of balance in your personality, parts of yourself that have been overstressed or undervalued. They can therefore point you towards all kinds of new growth: more profound self-understanding, self-acceptance and inner reconciliation; the healing of resentments, hurts, painful memories, broken relationships; new purpose and direction in your life.

In the prayer-relationship, God uses your dreams. Occasionally you can recognise with the greatest clarity that a particular dream is God's way of speaking to you. The Bible is full of examples of the way God communicates through dreams. God visited Abimelech in a dream at night.[17] God said to Solomon in a dream at Gibeon, 'Ask what you would like me to give you'.[18] On several occasions around the birth of Jesus, Joseph met an angel of the Lord in his dreams, who warned him and explained things to him.[19] And at Jesus' trial, Pilate's wife sent the message, 'Have nothing to do with that man; I have been upset all day by a dream I had about him.'[20]

The wisdom of the unconscious makes itself known to you also in your day-dreams, the idle, fragmented thoughts that flit through your mind and cause you to ask, 'Where did that come from?' When you learn to pay attention to those thoughts, you find that time after time they give you new insight into your unconscious relationship with God. Slips of the tongue can also be good clues to what is happening in your unconscious, those so-called Freudian slips that reveal things about you of which you were not aware, or which you thought were well hidden.

## The Persona

Jesus condemned as play-acting, hypocrisy, any religious actions that merely go through the motions for the sake of convention or respectability, or to satisfy our own selfish needs. 'In your prayers do not babble as the pagans do, for they think that by using many words they will make themselves heard. Do not be like them.'[21] 'When you pray, do not imitate the hypocrites: they love to say their prayers standing up in the synagogues and at the street corners for people to see them.'[22]

It is clear from the Gospels that Jesus was well aware of what we call the persona, a word derived from the masks which Greek actors wore to become 'dramatis personae'. Society expects you to play a part, to take your proper role in life as, for instance, a minister, a mother, a motor-mechanic, or a 'very model of a modern Major-General'.

Your mask allows you to play a role in society that is recognisable, predictable and therefore reliable. It protects your ego from the outer world. The danger is that you can confuse your persona with your real self. You can fail to see the real person behind your mask and come to believe that you are what you pretend to be. In his teaching on prayer, Jesus constantly urges you to go behind the superficial mask of your persona and expose your vulnerable and hidden self to God.

'When you pray, go to your private room and, when you have shut your door, pray to your Father who is in that secret place.'[23] The secret place is your heart, the hidden Self in the depths of your being, where God is to be found, where he 'sees all that is done in secret' knowing your need before you ask him.

## Projection

Jesus told a parable about two men who went up to the Temple to pray, one very religious, a Pharisee, and the other not very religious, a tax collector. The Pharisee

> 'stood there and said this prayer to himself, "I thank you God, that I am not grasping, unjust, adulterous like the rest of mankind, and particularly that I am not like this tax collector here. I fast twice a week; I pay tithes on all I get." The tax collector stood some distance away, not daring even to raise his eyes to heaven; but he beat his breast and said, "God, be merciful to me, a sinner".'

Jesus went on to say,

> 'This man . . . went home again at rights with God; the other did not. For everyone who exalts himself will be humbled, but the man who humbles himself will be exalted.'[24]

This parable shows Jesus' extraordinary perception of human personality. He knew that humility is impossible without self-knowledge. The tax collector was painfully looking into the depths of his life and confessing his sinfulness, while the Pharisee was so totally caught up with his own persona of the good, law-abiding and religious man, that it cast a dense Shadow that he was incapable of seeing. There, in his unconscious Shadow personality, were the vices of meanness, injustice and lust, projected by him on to the tax collector whom he saw as grasping, unjust and adulterous.

In the same way you and I unconsciously cast others in the light of our own unacknowledged feelings. You project on to others the parts of yourself that you dislike, disown and refuse to recognise. You dump your own prejudices, hatreds and anger on to others, disliking and despising them for what in reality should be owned by you. Jews, Blacks, Catholics, Protestants, Workers, Conservatives, Southerners, Women Priests – these and many other groups can be the objects on which you project your own unrecognised and unresolved problems. Whenever anyone or any group of people arouses very strong emotions in you, you must strongly suspect that your own Shadow personality has been touched. It is perhaps worth noting here that people who are extremely religious are very prone to projection. The preacher who noted in the margin of his sermon, 'Argument weak – shout!' was consciously stating what you unconsciously do whenever, from an attitude of apparent complete certainty, you fear, despise or attack those who disagree with you.

People are often not as you imagine them to be, especially when you find them irritating, hateful or despicable, because the chances are that you are seeing in them Shadow parts of yourself that need to be brought to light for healing.

## Facing the Shadow

'It is highly moral people,' Jung said, 'unaware of their other side, who develop particularly hellish moods which make them insupportable to their relatives'.[25] Perhaps that is why the common false caricature of a saint is of someone who would be impossible to live with. A famous Roman Catholic layman, Baron von Hugel, was once asked what qualities the Church looked for when canonising saints. He replied, 'Four things: loyalty to the faith, heroism in time of testing, power to do the apparently impossible, and, fourthly, radiance amidst the storm and stress of life.' Then he added, 'The church may conceivably have been wrong about the first three things, but it is gloriously right about the fourth.'[26] The ability to face with radiant honesty the dark side of life, uncover hidden motives, and so come to terms with the Shadow personality, is a mark of true sanctity.

In the first chapter I mentioned that my journey led me in adolescence through what I called 'shamefully intolerant excesses' of extreme Anglo-Catholicism. For a few years my new-found faith led me to depths of bigotry the remembrance of which still make me flush with remorse. I simply could not abide Protestants, and I despised and sneered at members of the Christian Union, the Salvation Army, Methodists – indeed at anyone who did not share my passion for all things Catholic. My frequent and punctilious examination of conscience and visits to my confessor never seemed to reveal the destructive prejudice that lay behind my fervent religious activity.

I now know that I was caught up in the problem of my dissociated, unacknowledged Shadow. Turning to face my Shadow has been a long, painful and vitally necessary struggle and it is not over yet. Bringing the darkness of your heart and mind to the light of Christ is a lifelong task. The great spiritual writers have always recognised that. So, for instance, the fourteenth-century author of the *Ladder of Perfection*, Walter Hilton, writes about the 'dark and painful image of your own soul. . . You carry about this image and black shadow with you wherever you go.'[27]

*Joan's Story*

A woman (we will call her Joan) in her fifties came to me with a problem. For the whole of her adult life she had tried very hard to be a good Christian – virtuous, happy, pure, kind and gentle, invariably patient and sympathetic, constantly loving and for-giving.

Joan told me that she could no longer pray. In fact she had no desire to pray. The well had run dry. She found herself becoming increasingly short-tempered, but tried not to show it. She said that she felt 'angry inside' and that her faith was just about dead. To add to her troubles, she was plagued by a constant nagging feeling of inadequacy and guilt, a persistent mild depression and a lack of energy and enthusiasm for life.

In the traditional Church of England Holy Communion service which Joan attended each Sunday morning, the general confession summed up her general feeling about herself: 'We acknowledge and bewail our manifold sins and wickednesses, Which we, from time to time, most grievously have committed, By thought, word, and deed, Against thy Divine Majesty, Provoking most justly thy wrath and indignation against us. . . The remembrance of them is grievous unto us; The Burden of them is intolerable. . .' Yet when Joan examined her conscience she could never discover anything really wicked, but always the same list of trivial peccadilloes, most of them arising from her tired and depressed state.

Joan had been so occupied with living out her ego-ideal, trying hard to be a good Christian, that she was denying in herself the reality of her Shadow personality. Her unconscious refusal to accept the fact of her Shadow was at the root of Joan's spiritual paralysis. The beginning of her healing had to be the fearful recog-nition in herself of the very opposites of all that she desired to be: evil desires, impurity, hatred, anger, jealousy, unforgiveness, intolerance, and much more.

My suggestion that she might find it helpful to discover more about her own personality by attending a Myers-Briggs workshop was met with resistance. That was not altogether surprising, as people who deny the reality of their Shadow will often resist any-thing that could open up the can of worms that they dare not acknowledge within themselves. In Joan's case, however, her reluctance was reinforced by a book she had found on her church bookstall that urged preoccupation with God rather than with self. The book mentioned the Myers-Briggs indicator in a disparaging way, confusing the struggle to know and understand oneself with a spiritual navel-gazing that is fundamentally self-absorbed, selfish and devoid of any social concern. The author followed a tendency among some modern Christian writers to view the quest for self-knowledge and self-realisation with deep suspicion, caricaturing it as 'egotistical' and 'narcissistic'.

Gradually, however, Joan came to see that her aim of 'self-forgetfulness' by means of a preoccupation with God is as danger-ously unbalanced as is a self-indulgent concern with one's own ego. I discussed with her the thought that if she was not in touch with her psychological processes, the god with whom she was pre-occupied may not be God at all, but an idol, created in her own image. Pursuing the goal of self-forgetfulness might, on the face of it, seem an attractive way of coping with the tensions and dishar-mony in her life. The danger was that it would lead to further denial of the unconscious Shadow part of herself which, if not confronted and brought into the light of God's grace, would con-tinue to exercise a destructive influence on her personality. The balanced way, I argued, is neither self-abnegation nor self-absorp-tion, but the proper use of all means at our disposal to become what we are, to be good stewards of the precious gift of self which God gives to each one of us. Growth in self-knowledge is a long, slow, arduous and often intensely painful task that leads, not to selfishness or egotism, but to an increasingly genuine openness to God. The ultimate goal is not self-improvement or psychological 'individuation', but a union of love with God and with one another, when we shall be our true selves and shall know as we are known.

I pointed out to Joan that self-knowledge and genuine openness to God, far from being mutually exclusive, belong together and that there are strong strands of classic Christian spirituality that testify to that. For instance, the fourteenth-century author of the *Cloud of Unknowing* tells us to 'swink and sweat in all that thou can'st and mayest for to get thee a true knowing and feeling of thyself as thou art. And then I trow soon after that thou wilt get thee a true knowing and feeling of God as he is.'[28] St Teresa of Avila considered self-knowledge 'so important that, even if you were raised right up to the heavens, I should like you never to relax your cultivation of it.'[29]

Joan came to see that the Christian profession is about *being* before it is about *doing* – being herself, being genuine before God, hiding nothing from herself or from God. Self-consciousness, self-awareness and self-understanding are, in Christian terms, gifts to help us respond to God's grace. Through them God loves us into life and draws us to himself so that we can *be* truly ourselves. Joan was putting up a good front, professing Christian beliefs, going to church, trying to lead a good life. But deep down it felt hollow, even hypocritical. More and more insistently Jesus' stern words to the scribes and Pharisees echoed in her mind: 'Alas for you. . . You who are like whitewashed tombs that look handsome on the outside, but inside are full of dead men's bones and every kind of corruption. In the same way you appear to people from the outside like good honest men, but inside you are full of hypocrisy and lawlessness.'[30]

Joan eventually attended a Myers-Briggs workshop and indicated INFP as her personality type. A new self-awareness began to dawn and with it, for the first time in her life, an appreciation of herself as a gift from God. Aspects of herself that she had always intuitively sensed but could not describe, she could now name with her new Myers-Briggs vocabulary. She discovered how her dominant function, introverted Feeling judgement, showed itself in a quiet, reserved attitude that masked a vulnerable inner tenderness. She could clearly recognise her gift of Intuitive perception with which she faced the world, and which gave her the ability and the urge to find, in her very open, flexible 'P' way, a purpose and pattern in her life.

Joan quickly grasped the truth that her conscious, egocentric 'self' was merely a tiny part of her real Self. With the preacher of Ecclesiastes she could say, 'Reality lies beyond my grasp; and deep, so deep, who can discover it?'[31] Her tertiary Sensing function and, most significantly, her inferior Thinking function became her passport to an adventure of discovery in the vast unexplored Holy Land of her unconscious life.

She began to pray again, and to pray differently, without pressure or anxiety about putting on a good show for God. She entered a new and exciting period of conversion.

Prayer for Joan had been like a tranquilliser, suppressing the pain that needed to be healed. Now she had new-found courage to be vulnerable, to surrender herself to God by turning to Christ with her whole being.

Joan began to face with God her Shadow personality, which was dominated by her vulnerable Thinking and Sensing functions. Deliberately she turned more and more to pray in her Shadow, using what I later describe as 'blue' and 'green' prayer, the colours opposite those of her dominant F and auxiliary N gifts.

The centre of her real Self was God, drawing her into fullness of life, impressing upon her the need to integrate her fragmented personality. That Self was showing her the paradoxical way to her self-fulfilment, drawing Joan to self-abandonment and self-giving love.

## Self-Fulfilment

Aspects of Joan's story will probably ring true in your own story. You may be able to see how the action of God in your life has at some time taken on a new insistence and intensity that you cannot resist without doing violence to your true Self.

God's will for you is a Self-fulfilment that is the very opposite of selfishness. You cannot become your true self without becoming God-centred, and that demands of you the faith and courage of self-sacrifice. There is no easy, pain-free road.

> Batter my heart, three-person'd God; for you
> As yet but knocke, breathe, shine, and seeke to mend;
> That I may rise, and stand, o'erthrow mee, 'and bend
> Your force, to breake, blowe, burn and make me new.
> . . . for I/Except you'enthrall mee, never shall be free,
> Nor ever chast, except you ravish mee.[32]

Turning to face your Shadow, and discovering that it is not a demon or a fearful ogre, but is a potentially life-enhancing part of you, is immensely liberating. When you turn your face to the sun, says the Maori proverb, the shadow falls behind you. As you grow in Christ, following him and opening your life more and more faithfully to 'the light of the world', the Shadow loses its negative and hostile grip on you, so that you no longer 'walk in the dark' but will 'have the light of life'.[33]

Every aspect of your personality, your experience, your responses to life's demands and challenges, has to go to and through the Cross and be redeemed by Christ. That Way of the Cross is the only road into the Kingdom of God. But it is not a lonely road, for you are always in the company of your brothers and sisters, walking together with Christ.

When Christ lives in your heart through faith you have strength to face your Shadow and grasp the reality of God's love empowering the hidden Self of your unconscious.

May God's Spirit give you the power

for your hidden self to grow strong, so that Christ may live in
your hearts through faith, and then, planted in love and built on
love, you will with all the saints have strength to grasp the
breadth and the length, the height and the depth; until, knowing
the love of Christ, which is beyond all knowledge, you are filled
with the utter fullness of God.[34]

# 5

# Living Images of God

The supreme expression of personality is God himself. Human beings are created in the image and likeness of God. Higher than the angels, we share the nature of the Divine.

All Christian prayer is incarnational. That is to say, it is a relationship with the one true God whose glory is disclosed and whose nature is embodied in the humanity of Jesus Christ. Jesus Christ is the living Word through whom the Creator made all things. By the power of the Holy Spirit the Word of God 'took flesh . . . born of the blessed Virgin, was seen on earth and went about among us.'[1]

The incarnation proclaims to us the extremity of God's outpouring, self-giving love for creation. It reveals God's humility towards us. In the incarnation, God's grace and truth was made manifest in human life. In the fullest possible way within the limitations of human personality, Jesus is the image of the invisible God. The Word Incarnate is a visual language for God.

The miracle of the incarnation opens the way for the fullness of life that is God's desire and gift for each one of us. 'The Word of God, Jesus Christ', wrote St Irenaeus, 'on account of His great love for humankind, became what we are in order to make us what He is himself.' 'We shall be like him.'[2] Jesus Christ who shared our human nature has made us co-heirs of his divine nature. We have the capacity to disclose God, to become 'other Christs' in the world. That capacity is *the* distinguishing mark of a human being.

'It's all gift!' Baron von Hügel used to say. All that you have, all that you are, all that you can ever hope to be is derived from the God in whose image you are created, giving you your dignity and uniqueness.

Human maturity is measured by 'growing into the full stature of love and knowledge in the power and grace of God.'[3] The letter to the Ephesians speaks of growing 'in all ways into Christ, who is the head by whom the whole body is fitted and joined together, every joint adding its own strength, for each separate part to work according to its function. So the body grows until it has built itself up, in love.'[4]

The ultimate goal of this growth is corporate. Together we become perfect Humanity, 'fully mature with the fullness of Christ himself.' Your individual pilgrimage towards human maturity is a tiny but vital movement within the body as together, from glory to glory advancing, we grow into the image of God in Christ.

The more we can see the image of God reflected in every single individual, the more we will recapture a sense of the inherent beauty and creativity of human personality. People are precious not because of their utility, but because they reflect the image of the Divine. They are like God. That likeness can be seen in each of the gifts of personality described in the previous chapters.

## The Extravert God

Your ability to extravert is a gift from God. The God who delights to pour love, creative energy, outwards to form and hold in existence the material universe is an extravert God.

When extraverting, you remember, the process is visible, 'out there'. The E God is revealed through external things – Scripture, the natural world, the events of history, your bodily life. God is open and accessible, knowable by anyone who has eyes to see and ears to hear, and he shares his E nature with you.

> Yes, naturally stupid are all men who have not
>   known God
> and who, from the good things that are seen, have not been
>   able to discover Him-who-is,
> or, by studying the works, have failed to
>   recognise the Artificer.
> . . . through the grandeur and beauty of the creatures we may,
> by analogy, contemplate their Author.[5]

You can glimpse the mystery of God through the created universe. The wonders uncovered by the discoveries of chemist, physicist, and every other kind of scientist speak of God. Creation is good, for it is God's vehicle and glory. 'He who sees the world in God stands in God's presence', said Martin Buber. Psalm 19, among many others, celebrates the E character of God: 'The heavens declare the glory of God, the vault of heaven proclaims his handiwork.'

The extravert God is immanent in his creation, personally energising every moment of its existence and loving every living creature into life. You meet the E God in other people, and as you worship in the fellowship of believers you can rejoice that your ability to extravert is a gift and reflection of God.

## The Introvert God

You can also see in the very being of God, the I gift. Whenever you introvert, you focus your life energy within yourself. The energy of God's life and love is discovered within the divine mystery of the Holy Trinity, Creator and Redeemer united in love by the Holy Spirit. Eternally the Divine Life is a relationship of mutual self-giving. God is self-sufficient and does not 'need' creation. The interior life of God is utterly beyond our comprehension, rich beyond our imagining and the source of our own ability to introvert.

The I God is transcendent, unknowable and inaccessible. You meet and celebrate the introvert God in solitude and silence. He is revealed through the 'still small voice' within, through inspiration, personal visions and enlightenment. 'Be still and know that I am God.'[6]

## The Sensing God

The S God is reflected in all human personality. Sensing is the gift of being able to perceive through sight, touch, taste, smell and hearing. It is the gift of detailed, immediate awareness of things as they are.

God is the God of all that is real to the senses, from the macro to the micro, from the galaxies to the minutest particle of matter. God joyfully creates the sun and the moon, the snowflake and the stork, the Korean hanging bellied pig and the dolphin, and delights to share his S gift with his creatures. Whenever you use the S function by being observant, detailed, practical, down-to-earth, realistic, sensible, sensual, you are imaging your Creator.

Voltaire once said that men and women were created in God's own image and they have been returning the compliment ever since. In their concern not to think of God in human terms and make him an idol in their own image, Christians have sometimes denied that the material, sensual gifts are really of God. Contrary to the earthy, creationist biblical revelation and the truth of the incarnation, they have tried to dematerialise and spiritualise God. But God is in no way less than human. 'Is the inventor of the ear unable to hear? The creator of the eye unable to see?'[7]

God listens attentively when you speak. God calls you by name, numbers the hairs of your head, and notes each sparrow that falls to the ground.

The time focus of the S gift is the 'here-and-now', and God's time is the present. Now is the acceptable time, now is the moment of salvation.[8]

God comes to us in the S way of simplicity. Revealed in human flesh, born of a woman, he trod this earth with us and died his death for us.

## The Intuitive God

Who imagined the unimaginable? Who dreamed up the created universe? The visionary N God is never afraid to take risks, perceiving eternally new patterns and possibilities, always finding the creative way through any problem. God is the mysterious and hidden God, revealed in symbol, allusion and paradox.

The N God forever intuits new ways of showing love, recreating, renewing, and restoring a fallen world so that God's Realm will come on earth as it is in heaven.

The intuitive God has an infinity of ways to achieve the purposes of love. Nothing is impossible to God. Jeremiah heard God say, 'See, I am Yahweh . . . is anything impossible to me?'[9]

When Jesus told the disciples that it is as hard for those who have riches to enter the Kingdom of God as it is for a camel to pass through the eye of a needle, the disciples said to one another, 'In that case who can be saved?' 'For men,' Jesus said, 'this is impossible; for God everything is possible.'[10]

Sarah, well past the age of child-bearing, laughed at the very idea that she might have a son. Yahweh asked Abraham, 'Why did Sarah laugh . . . ? Is anything too wonderful for Yahweh?',[11] words echoed by the Angel Gabriel when Mary asked, 'But how can this come about?'[12]

The N time focus is towards what might be. It is always looking at what is to come. It is the N God of the future who 'has let us know the mystery of his purpose, the hidden plan he so kindly made in Christ from the beginning to act upon when the times had run their course to the end; that he would bring everything together under Christ, as head, everything in the heavens and everything on earth.'[13]

## The Thinking God

Whenever you use your T gift of logical, rational judgement, you reflect the nature of a God who is righteous, faithful and true. The T God, 'who is faithful and just will forgive our sins and purify us from everything that is wrong.'[14]

Your ability to be objective, to take a long cool look at the evidence and judge accordingly, derives from the T God who is infinitely just and totally impartial. 'God has no favourites'.[15] The

God of gods and Lord of lords is King of the ages, whose ways are just and true.

God is utterly trustworthy, your ruler, lawgiver and absolute judge. The character of the T God is truth, consistency, reason and wisdom. 'How rich are the depths of God – how deep his wisdom and knowledge – and how impossible to penetrate his motives or understand his methods! Who could ever know the mind of the Lord?'[16]

You can dispute and argue with God, who is consistent, never fickle or unreasonable. In fact, our very insistence that God should be God, and display a passionate justice, is in itself a reflection in us of the T image of God. Abraham interceded for Sodom demanding justice of God: 'to kill the just man with the sinner, treating just and sinner alike? Do not think of it! Will the judge of the whole earth not administer justice?'[17]

When you confront God with honest doubts, arguing and reasoning with the Divine, you are reflecting the Thinking image of God.

## The Feeling God

The F God 'knows your hearts'[18] and is the God who feels the world's pain and shares your sufferings. 'God comforts the miserable';[19] indeed Paul describes him as 'the God of all comfort'.[20] The Feeling God is the great encourager, who longs for us to live in harmony with one another,[21] to agree with one another and live in peace.[22] Five times in the New Testament God is described as 'the God of peace'. The longing of F judgement to create a happy, peaceful and harmonious society is an image of that F God who 'is not a God of confusion but of peace'.[23]

There is nothing weak or sentimental about the F image of God – no question of being swayed by emotion. All goodness is of God, as Jesus said, 'No one is good but God alone'.[24] The God of hope fills you with all joy and peace in believing,[25] and rejoices over you. The angels of our F God rejoice over one repentant sinner.[26]

T-judgement and F-judgement are held together by God in a way which we humans, at our best, long and strive for but rarely attain. In God 'mercy and truth are met together; righteousness and peace have kissed each other.'[27] Often in the Old Testament, twenty-three times in the Psalms alone, God is described by a Hebrew word that no single English word can translate. It is the word *chesed*, which in the richness of its meaning embraces the T and the F character of God, and the T and F gifts in human personality. Psalm 86:15 describes this T–F God: 'Lord God, you who are always merciful and tender-hearted, slow to anger, always loving, always loyal.' *Chesed* includes faithfulness, trustworthiness, truthfulness, loyalty, righteousness, mercy, kindness, long-suffering, compassion, tenderness, and pity.

Human beings reflect the image of the God of Love in an F way as well as a T way. 'Note then the kindness and the severity of God', Paul writes,[28] the F and T sides of the same coin.

## The Judging God

When you use your Judging function and display the J attitude, wanting closure, decisiveness, structure and order, you reflect the image of the J God. The Judging God brings order out of chaos, demonstrating 'the unchangeable character of his purpose.' His very word is an act of creation that always achieves what it proclaims.[29] He speaks, and it is done.

Yahweh does not 'hobble first on one leg then on the other',[30] unlike the people of Israel who were unwilling to close their options. 'If Yahweh is God', Elijah told them, 'follow him; if Baal, follow him.' God does not vacillate. He is not fickle or uncertain. Our J God judges, decides, chooses, calls, acts. Solomon's prayer was to the judging nature of God: 'Hear from heaven, . . . act, decide . . .'[31]

The J God lays before us choices and decisions. 'I set before you life or death, blessing or curse. Choose life, then, so that you and your descendants may live, in the love of Yahweh your God, obeying his voice, clinging to him.'[32] Stability, order, reliability, discernment, sound judgement, trustworthiness are human virtues that reflect the J God who urges you not to look back once your hand is laid on the plough.[33]

## The Perceiving God

Whenever you adopt the P attitude, you are reflecting the image of One who is infinitely open, receptive and spontaneous. God is not inflexible. That lovely story of Abraham persuading God to change his mind about the destruction of Sodom – 'will you not spare the place for the fifty just men in it?'[34] – is just one of the many biblical illustrations of the Perceiving character of God.

God's judgement is never hasty. He is always 'slow to anger'.[35] The enquiring, open-minded P attitude in human personality images the God who listens, observes, and waits patiently for us.

When you are being open to whatever life offers, curious, spontaneous, fun-loving, you are reflecting the ebullient God of delight and joy, who laughs and plays and enjoys creation, the P God in whom there is an endless sabbath rest.

## Jesus – The One for All Types

I am often asked what type I think Jesus was, and I usually answer provocatively, 'He was an introverted, intuitive feeling type, of course, an INFJ!'

We all like to see our own type in Jesus. We see in him the strengths and preferences of our own personality, and so think of him as a perfect representative of our own type.

At other times, though, I think of Jesus as the type of my Shadow personality, ESTP. Those parts of myself that I find difficult and weak, I sometimes admire and sometimes find irritating in other people, but I see them as strengths in the person of Jesus.

So, if each of us recognises his or her own personality type in Jesus, do we conclude that the incarnate Son of God was none (or all) of the sixteen types? Probably not, for Jesus was a real man, truly human, and it is difficult to see how that could be if he was not only of a particular gender, race, physical build, genetic make-up, but also a particular personality type.

In the mercy of God, however, we do not know Jesus' type and have no way of discovering it, for each of the four evangelists has his own type bias in presenting the gospel. As we will see, they are a T, S, F and N bias respectively.

Whatever type Jesus was, he lived it perfectly. In the person of Jesus we glimpse what it means to grow fully into the gifts of human personality. He is the model for all Christians of the integrated and individuated person. Our task is to employ our own gifts of personality to grow together into a new humanity, 'fully mature with the fullness of Christ himself.'[36]

*Four Gospels – Four Functions*

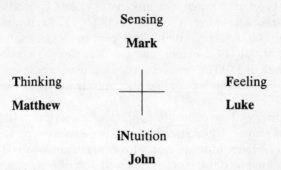

Sensing

**Mark**

Thinking            Feeling

**Matthew**         **Luke**

iNtuition

**John**

Christ wrote no book; he left in the world as His witness a 'body' of men and women upon whom His Spirit came. There was to be nothing stereotyped. The living society – the Church – was to be the primary witness. The Gospels were written by members of the Church for their fellow-members, and each is 'The Gospel according to' somebody. What reaches us is never a certified record but always a personal impression. Thus our concern is always with the Christ of faith, not with some supposed different Jesus of history. It is by the faith of others that our faith is kindled, even when that other is a Synoptic Evangelist.[37]

The books we call the four Gospels were a completely new genre. They are not biography or history, as we think of biography and history today. Rather, they are the proclamation of good news (which is what the word 'gospel' means) concerning God's personal intervention in human history through the life, ministry, death and resurrection of Jesus Christ.

All four Gospels are composed of independent units of material, stories about Jesus, the teachings of Jesus, accounts of the Passion, and so on. These were passed down during the first decades of the Church's life and worship, collected by the evangelists, and arranged and edited by them in the form we have them now in our New Testament.

Each evangelist had a different audience in mind, and each presented the Good News in his own personal way, as he was inspired by the Holy Spirit. The evangelists' own type preferences colour the selection, arrangement and editing of the material in their Gospels.

Most Christians have their favourite of the four Gospels, though it is important to understand that your favourite may not be the one that corresponds to your favourite function. In terms of personality type, like sometimes attracts like, and opposites sometimes attract each other. There is, thank God, no rule about it. In marriage, for instance, there is a certain amount of flocking together of birds of a feather, and most couples share at least two letters in their MBTI types. Nevertheless, there are many happily married people who are completely opposite in type to their partners.

This brings us again to the dangers of prescription in relating type and prayer. Understanding your personality type will never give you a blueprint for prayer. However, it will give you greater understanding and tolerance of yourself and of others, and many helpful clues to lead you towards a more integrated prayer relationship.

## Mark – The Sensing Gospel

It is generally accepted that Mark is the earliest of the four Gospels, written in the period AD 45–70.

It shows many S characteristics, such as simplicity. The construction of Mark's Gospel lacks the patterns and complexities of the other three Gospels. It simply begins with the baptism and temptation of Jesus and his ministry in Galilee, Judea, Jerusalem, and concludes with a long and detailed account of the Lord's passion, death and resurrection.

Mark was a born story-teller, a frequent S characteristic. He always had the S focus on the immediate moment. The historic present tense appears no less than 151 times in his short Gospel, and that little S word *euthus*, meaning 'immediately', 'straightway', or 'at once', occurs forty-two times, giving a sense of sequence from one event to the next.

Greek is clearly not his mother tongue. Nevertheless, its rough and ready, straightforward, vigorous style, brief and to the point, is typically S.

Mark's Gospel has the flavour of vivid eye-witness reports. For instance, 'In the morning, long before dawn, he got up and left the house, and went off to a lonely place and prayed there.'[38]

Many people think that Mark was Peter's disciple and interpreter, and that he was the John Mark whose mother's house was used by the early church.[39] It is also quite possible that he was the young man mentioned only in Mark's Gospel, who 'had nothing on but a linen cloth. They caught hold of him, but he left the cloth in their hands and ran away naked.'[40] It is difficult to imagine why Mark included that detail unless it had a personal significance for him. In any case, the inclusion of such detail is a clear S characteristic of the kind that appears throughout Mark's Gospel.

Although he writes more briefly and less elegantly than the other evangelists, he often includes vivid sensory details that they omit. It is as though he 'sees' what he is writing. He describes Jesus listening, gazing, touching. Time and again he tells of Jesus restoring the gifts of the senses, healing the blind, the deaf, the dumb.

In the story of the stilling of the storm, only Mark gives the visual image of Jesus asleep 'in the stern, his head on the cushion' and Jesus' words to the sea, 'Quiet now! Be calm!'[41] It is only from Mark that we know how Jesus felt when the woman with a haemorrhage touched him; he was 'immediately aware that power had gone out from him.'[42] Mark, but not the other evangelists, tells us that Jesus 'put his arms round' the little children,[43] that when the rich young man knelt before him, Jesus 'looked steadily at him and loved him', and the young man's 'face fell . . . and he went away sad.'[44] In Mark alone we learn that the grass on which the multitude sat was 'green'.[45]

These and many other graphic details are a feature of Mark's Gospel, helping to give it an essentially S quality.

## Matthew – The Thinking Gospel

Matthew, on the other hand, gives us a much longer and more systematic account, particularly of Christ's teaching.

The T gift is concerned with logical order and argument, factual analysis, objective principles and truth. These T characteristics are found most clearly in the Gospel according to Matthew.

Written probably by a Jewish Christian, Matthew's is the most carefully planned and structured of the four Gospels. Five collections of the sayings of Jesus, all ending with a formula such as 'Jesus had now finished what he wanted to say',[46] parallel the five books of Moses known as the Pentateuch.

Furthermore, the Gospel divides clearly into seven parts. There are seven parables in chapter 13 and seven 'Woes' in chapter 23. Matthew also seems to like threes, as in the three angelic messages to Joseph and the three denials by Peter. His precise mind clearly enjoyed arranging his material, often in a certain order called a *chiasmus*, a,b:b,a.

In chapters 5–7 Matthew gives us the Sermon on the Mount that parallels the Old Testament experience on Mount Sinai. He portrays Jesus as the new Moses who gives the new law of Christ to the New Israel, the Church. All the T concerns for law, justice and true judgement are reflected in his favourite word 'righteousness'.

The Jesus of Matthew is the Lord, the Christ, the King of Israel, the Son of God, whose claim on humanity is total. Jesus is to be followed and obeyed, because he is the one who reveals truth, who judges justly, who rewards and punishes. He it is who 'will clear his threshing-floor and gather his wheat into the barn; but the chaff he will burn in a fire that will never go out.'[47] For Matthew, the Good News has clear and inescapable implications for faith and obedience.

Of all the evangelists, Matthew lays most stress on the fulfilment of the Scriptures in Jesus. Ten times Matthew adds to his main source, the earlier Gospel of Mark, quotations from the Old Testament with the formula, 'Now all this took place to fulfil the words spoken by the Lord through the prophet.'[48]

So we can see in Matthew's Gospel a clear T concern for things to make sense. He wanted to arrange and structure his book in a systematic and logical way.

Ts, with their ability to focus on the objective truth in any situation, can handle conflict well. Matthew, more than the other three Gospels, shows Jesus in conflict with his enemies and handling that conflict in an unambiguous, honest and dignified manner, with total authority and self-control.


## Luke – The Feeling Gospel

Luke was also the author of the Acts of the Apostles and so over a quarter of the New Testament comes from his hand. There is a tradition that Luke was a painter, and a doctor, the 'beloved physician' of Colossians 4:14.

The F gifts include intimacy, gratitude, empathy, healing and harmony, all of which are characteristic of Luke's Gospel.

Luke is the Gospel of the poor. He shows a special concern for the outcast, the downtrodden, and the oppressed. His account of the anointing of Jesus in the Pharisee's house by an immoral woman is beautiful and touching, with its emphasis on uncalculating love: 'I tell you that her sins, her many sins, must have been forgiven her, or she would not have shown such great love. It is the man who is forgiven little who shows little love.'[49]

Luke's F-judgement urges him to stress Jesus' innocence of the crimes of which he was accused and condemned. He tells us that Pilate repeatedly said that Jesus was not guilty and that he could find no case against him.[50]

Fs dislike excluding people. They will always look for any reasons, excuses and mitigating circumstances to include people. We see this tendency in Luke's universalism, which is absent in the other three. For instance, the whole human race is included in Luke's genealogy of Jesus. Whereas Matthew gives Jesus' ancestry back to Abraham, father of the Jewish nation, Luke traces it back to Adam, father of humankind. We also see in Luke a concern to show that the gospel has broken down barriers between man and woman, Jew and Gentile.

Luke sees the love and salvation of God extended through the gospel of Jesus to Gentiles, foreigners, social outcasts, sinners, the poor, the maimed, the lame, the blind – all are given places of honour in the feast of God's Kingdom.

The gender distinction between the T and F preferences is highlighted in Luke's Gospel, where women play a much more noticeable and important role than in the other three Gospels. The Jesus of Luke has strong feeling judgement. He stands in the midst of people, feels for them, shares their concerns and sympathises with their weaknesses.

Without Luke we would never have heard of the parable of the Lost Son,[51] which speaks of a God of love who is always there for us with open arms, waiting to embrace us and rejoice over us, with no recriminations or demands, whenever we come to our senses and repent. Among other characteristically F parables recorded only in Luke are those of the Good Samaritan, the Pharisee and the Publican, and the Rich Fool.

We have to turn to Luke to find the lovely story of Zacchaeus, the rich publican, in which Jesus says of himself, 'the Son of Man has come to seek out and save what was lost.'[52] Luke alone records the incident with Mary and Martha,[53] and the words from the Cross to the penitent thief, 'I promise you, today you will be with me in paradise.'[54] Without our F evangelist we would know nothing of the meeting of the risen Lord with Cleopas and his companion on the road to Emmaus.[55] 'Did not our hearts burn within us,' they

said, 'as he talked to us on the road?' We could hardly find a
stronger F response than that.

Also distinctive to Luke are many references to Jesus at prayer,
in constant and trusting communion with his Father. 'He would
always go off to some place where he could be alone and pray.'[56]


## John – The Intuitive Gospel

Matthew, Mark and Luke are very alike, which is why they are
called the 'synoptic' Gospels. John, however, has little in common
with the synoptics. He wrote much later, possibly towards the end
of the first century, and his work is the result of deep theological
reflection. Often called the spiritual Gospel, it opens with a mag-
nificent Prologue[57] proclaiming Jesus as the creative Word of God
made flesh.

The N gift is the ability to gather information by way of allusion,
metaphor, poetry and symbolism. Words are often encased in layer
upon layer of meaning. Conceptual N words were favourites with
John: glory, truth, knowledge, regeneration, belief, word, life,
light, love, and many more.

The opposite S gift is the ability to be concise and to the point,
to tell stories and give factual accounts of events. In John we find
little of that. His Gospel contains not a single parable. There is no
account of the birth, baptism and temptation of Jesus, or of his
transfiguration. John does not mention Peter's profession of faith,
the Last Supper, Gethsemane, or the ascension.

What we do find in John are long, complex discourses, as
involved and thought-provoking as any N-preferring type could
desire. N perceptions dip in and out of the unconscious, gleaning
patterns and associations. Typically, they dot around and light on
this, and then on that, and then link that up with the other. William
Temple described that characteristic of John's mind in this way:
'He seems to say "look at A; now look at B; now look at AB; now
at C; now at BC; now at AC; now at D and E; now at ABE; now
at CE", and so on in any variety or combination that facilitates
new insight.'[58]

John's Gospel is a supreme example of God's gift to us of intuitive perception. The factual details of Jesus' life and death were of
interest to him only as they revealed the eternal meaning within
them. John always sought to uncover the significance of the historical events surrounding Jesus, to show the heavenly meaning of the

earthly story. He wanted his readers to see that in Jesus the saving purpose of God for creation was uniquely revealed. 'Grace and truth have come through Jesus Christ. No one has ever seen God; it is the only Son, who is nearest to the Father's heart, who has made him known.'[59]

In typically N fashion, John was always looking at the future implications and significances of the gospel. His focus was towards the ultimate fulfilment of God's purpose in Christ, the bliss of which all our present blessings are but a foretaste.

The life of Jesus was, for John, a window through which God's truth can be glimpsed. So the miracles, a blind man given sight, water changed to wine, Lazarus raised to life, are not wonder-working but powerful signs. Each miracle is followed by a long, abstract and often enigmatic discourse on its spiritual significance. The signs in John's Gospel manifest 'the glory of God in the face of Christ'[60] and 'are recorded so that you may believe that Jesus is the Christ, the Son of God, and that believing this you may have life through his name.'[61]

John, like all N-preferring people, loved to use imaginative symbols. So for instance, the Jesus of John is described in a series of 'I am' statements, each of which illuminated some aspect of the mystery of the Word made flesh: 'I am the bread of life', 'the light of the world', 'the door', 'the good shepherd', 'the resurrection and the life', 'the way, the truth and the life', 'the true vine'.

## Four Gospels – One Gospel

In the providence of God each of the four written Gospels is coloured by one of the four functions of personality, S, N, T, F. When the four of them are taken together, their words reveal the Word for all to hear.

# 6

## Praying Your Way

'Be happy at all times; pray constantly; and for all things give thanks to God, because this is what God expects you to do in Christ Jesus.'[1] Paul is not urging you to 'pray without ceasing', in the sense of trying to say prayers all the time or even of trying to be conscious of God all the time. He is reminding you that your relationship with God is an endless reality.

Constant prayer is a faithful love-relationship. Far from being an escape into romantic self-absorbed mystical experience, it is 'the responsibility to meet others with all that I have, . . . to expect to meet God in the way, not to turn aside from the way.'[2] 'Pray constantly' is an appeal to you to cast the light of the gospel over the whole of life, always and everywhere.

Praying your way through life is a journey towards God that you travel with an attitude of openness and a willingness to allow God continually to convert you. It means discovering the Self in yourself or, as Richard Foster describes it, living from the Centre. He writes,

> For years I loved him and sought to obey him, but he remained on the periphery of my life. God and Christ were extremely important to me but certainly not the Centre. . . I was deeply committed, but I was not integrated or unified. I thought that serving God was another duty to be added onto an already busy schedule. But slowly I came to see that God desired to be not on the outskirts but at the heart of my experience.[3]

To pray *your* way does not mean choosing what is congenial to you and discarding anything else. Praying your way means having the courage to face the truth about yourself and the faith to love yourself as a gift from God. It means learning to go with rather than against the grain of your personality. It also means desiring what God desires for you, which may or may not be what is at present congenial to you.

## Procrastination and Prayer

I remember a Confirmation preparation manual that contained a cartoon of a man holding a cup and saucer. The caption read, 'I was going to say my prayers, but I decided to have a cup of tea instead'.

Many of us want to devote time to God in prayer, but for some reason or the other find that we do not get around to it. We think about praying, we like the idea of praying, we plan our praying, we read about praying – and we end up by actually praying very little, if at all, in the sense of deliberately attending to God.

Some types, especially IN– – types, tend to be perfectionist. INFPs and INTPs are often fascinated by the whole idea of prayer. They collect books on the subject, dabble around in mysticism and spirituality, but find it difficult to engage in a disciplined, structured relationship with God.

Whatever INFJs and INTJs undertake, including prayer, has to be done really well. They need to learn that we relate to God *as we are*, not as we would ideally like to be. Pray as you can, not as you can't, was Dom Chapman's wise advice which all of us, but particularly INFJs and INTJs, should take to heart.

All the NT types, INTJ, INTP, ENTP and ENTJ, share a desire to understand and master whatever they tackle. However, full understanding and complete mastery applied to a relationship as mysterious as prayer is of course impossible. Procrastination for these types often takes the form of, 'I will start praying when I am really sure what prayer is.' Or, 'I cannot pray without compromising my intellectual integrity.' Or, 'I will pray when I am sure that what I am doing is theologically impeccable.' As we will see when we consider what I call blue prayer, T types can easily fail to recognise the prayer that is already there in their intellectual activity.

ISFPs and ISTPs may avoid setting aside time for prayer if it seems to them a relatively unpleasant activity. If they think of prayer as a stern duty imposed on them by God and the Church they will want to avoid it. They are spontaneous, adventurous people. Planned and predictable activities are often, for them, dull and boring.

The abstract is uninteresting for them, as it is also for the ESFP and ESTP types, who often procrastinate in a similar way. They get drawn away by any excitements of the moment that may be (and usually are) happening around them. Life, they say, is for living, not for sitting around being introspective and thinking fine thoughts. So they need to see that the prayer relationship is here, now, in this moment of time, wherever you are, whatever you are doing. It does not necessarily require withdrawal, abstraction.

All the –S–P types need to discover the excitement and fun in the venture of faith. They need to experience the concrete reality of God in their everyday lives. More than any of the other types, they have the gift of finding God in the sacrament of the present moment. The commonsense approach and advice given by Brother Lawrence in his book *The Practice of the Presence of God* often help the –S–P types overcome their prayer paralysis.

The ENFP and ENTP types, with their dominant extraverted intuition, and consequent inferior sensing, are frequently so full of alluring projects, ideas, people, that their well-intentioned prayer time becomes submerged in the welter of their activities. They can all too easily lose any sense of priority and any clarity about what is really important for them. I have often found, with people who indicate these types, that their best way into a disciplined relationship of prayer is through their auxiliary judging function. So the ENFP will usefully turn initially to red (Feeling) prayer, and the ENTP to blue (Thinking) prayer.

E– –J types (ESTJ, ENTJ, ESFJ and ENFJ) are in my experience the least likely to procrastinate about prayer. They are types who like to control life, and to do their duty in a competent and responsible way – and that includes prayer. However, they have their own typological problems. So much in the prayer relationship is about turning to God in the knowledge that we are weak, incompetent and out of control – a hard lesson for these E– –J types to learn. They, and the I– –Js too, often need to learn how to 'waste time' with God without feeling guilty.

## Prayer and Discipline

All prayer is response to God's grace at work in us. Our efforts in prayer depend upon God encouraging and enabling us to make the effort; but make it we must, if we would become what we have it in us to be.

Paul, in his second letter to Timothy, writes about the inevitability of hardship and the need for toughness in the Christian life.

Put up with your share of difficulties, like a good soldier of

Christ Jesus. In the army, no soldier gets himself mixed up in civilian life, because he must be at the disposal of the man who enlisted him; or take an athlete – he cannot win any crown unless he has kept all the rules of the contest; and again, it is the working farmer who has the first claim on any crop that is harvested. Think over what I have said, and the Lord will show you how to understand it all.[4]

That ability to face hardship is, for a Christian, not ego-generated but Self-generated in the sense of being empowered by the indwelling Christ.

## Self-control

Self-control is one of the lovely qualities of personality listed by Paul as the fruit of the Spirit: 'love, joy, peace, patience, kindness, goodness, trustfulness, gentleness and self-control'.[5] Those characteristics of the Spirit-directed life belong together as a unity. They are the fruit of the Spirit, not separate fruits of the Spirit. So the self-control that the Spirit brings to your life is not the stiff-upper-lip, men-don't-cry, cold-showers-are-good-for-you kind of self-discipline. As part of the fruit of the Spirit, it is a loving, joyful, peaceful, kind, good, trustful, gentle self-mastery which Christ alone can give.

'Accept the strength, my dear son', Paul writes, 'that comes from the grace of Christ Jesus.' And then he quotes the encouraging words of one of the earliest known Christian hymns:

> If we have died with him, then we shall live with him.
> If we hold firm, then we shall reign with him.
> If we disown him, then he will disown us.
> We may be unfaithful, but he is always faithful,
> for he cannot disown his own self.[6]

Prayer and discipline are inseparable because our pilgrimage is the way of Christ's self-giving love, the Way of the Cross. I remind you again that this is not a lonely pilgrimage. We tread the path of prayer in community. We are in fellowship with the People of God throughout the world and throughout time. In focusing on our individual relationship with God we must never forget the corporate context of all prayer.

Prayer is the most natural relationship in the world. That does not mean, however, that prayer is easy. Sin hinders prayer. Human beings are not automatons. You have the freedom to love, or to hate. You can respond with gratitude to the Giver of all good things, or you can behave like an ungrateful and selfish child. At every moment of life you can choose to face God, or to turn your back on God.

Any relationship, not least your prayer relationship with God, that is not undergirded by a tough, determined 'stickability' is very unlikely to flourish. Self-discipline is not the most popular virtue, but it is an essential prerequisite of any developed skill. Almost anything really life-enhancing demands from you practice and training. Prayer needs discipline and effort just as much as playing a musical instrument, painting, cabinet making, or speaking a foreign language.

## Habits

Discipline in prayer means constantly replacing old habits with new and better habits – habits of mind and thought, as well as habits of action. The society and culture that surround us help create our habits. A young man seeking the approval of his peers can easily learn the habits of foul language, heavy drinking, and of viewing every attractive woman he sees in a salacious way, mentally undressing her. As he grows older and wiser he may well desire to change his ways, but he will not find it easy. Old habits of life, speech and thought must be erased and new ones learnt. Determination, discipline and a different context of relationships for that young man are essential. Only then will he learn new habits of gentleness in language, moderation in drinking, and of seeing women as human beings rather than objects of selfish gratification.

We can want to see Christ in others. That is a lovely thought; but without a great deal of self-imposed training and discipline it will remain just that – a lovely thought. Really to see Christ in each person we meet requires a putting to death of old habits of competition, social stereotyping, the desire to dominate, impress, or make use of people.

Turning to God in prayer is hard work. Repentance and conversion are incessant imperatives throughout our pilgrimage. Self-examination and increasing self-knowledge are not optional extras, for 'whoever would enter God's ground, His inmost part, must first enter his own ground, his inmost part, for none can know God who does not first know himself.'[7]

## Effortless Delight

The wonderful paradox is that effortless delight intertwines your struggle as you receive glimpses of God. Behind all the effort and discipline of your prayer-relationship, the basic truth is that the Spirit alone gives life. Any growth comes only from God.[8] Discipline and training are ways in which you play your part and prepare the ground for the grace of God to germinate and bear fruit in your life. Without the grace of our Lord Jesus Christ, the love of God and the fellowship of the Holy Spirit, all the discipline and training in the world will produce nothing more than a legalistic religion directed towards your own pride and self-satisfaction.

## Your Image of God

Entering into a conscious relationship of prayer with God always gives energy. Is your prayer enervating or invigorating? If your praying bores, wearies or frustrates you, perhaps you should ask yourself whether you have got into a rut in your habits of prayer.

Strangely, people often cannot see the connection between problems in praying and growth in the knowledge of God. From time to time you will need, deliberately and sometimes painfully, to break out of old habits of prayer that have become lifeless or compulsive, so that you can renew your relationship with God. When such times of radical change come, it is particularly necessary to seek the support and guidance of a soul friend, spiritual guide, director, or some other companion on the way.

If you want to know what you really believe, examine the way you pray. Some people pray in childish forms throughout their lives. Their image of God is fixated in childhood. Your cultivation or neglect of a prayer-relationship with God and your expectations of that relationship will tell you more than anything else about what you truly believe. The other side of that coin is that the more clearly you come to understand the nature of God, the more clearly you will know what it means to pray. As you grow from a more idolatrous to a less idolatrous image of God you will inevitably need to change your prayer-relationship.

You may have a disturbing and unpleasant 'dark night' or 'tunnel-like' experience in which what once served you well in prayer no longer satisfies. It has become dry, hollow and meaningless. There are many possible explanations for that kind of experience, but frequently it seems that habitual patterns of prayer have over the years fossilised into an obsessive and Spirit-stifling legalism. They have become old wineskins that have lost their suppleness and can no longer be stretched. Prayer has become an anxious and guilt-laden relationship. You cannot base a living, loving relationship on anxiety about fulfilling ritual acts – even if that ritual act is 'My Quiet Time' or 'Saying my Office'. Your prayer relationship with God must never be allowed to become formalised, for then your habits of prayer are rooted not in God, but in your own need for security, or to be in control, or to justify yourself.

## Fallow Times

Whenever you respond to God in prayer, you become vulnerable to the Spirit and open to new direction. To discover that new direction sometimes requires of you drastic action. You may need to take a sabbatical rest from your prayer habits and routines. Occasionally (though clergy will find this difficult) you may even need a sabbatical rest from going to church, simply to reawaken your hunger for Word and Sacrament in the fellowship of believers. The point is that from time to time God requires of us a fallow period in which our prayer relationship can renew its fertility, and so flourish again with new vigour.

## Prayer and Self-knowledge

I have said that prayer and discipline are inseparable. I must add that prayer and self-knowledge are also inseparable. We need to cultivate a tough and demanding poverty of spirit before we can begin to know ourselves as God knows us. 'What a person is before God, that he or she is and nothing more', said St Francis of Assisi. Prayer differentiates the Self from the ego, and that is a hard and humbling process.

## Conditions for Growth

To help create the conditions for growth towards sanctity, the wholeness of being that we recognise as holiness, you must cultivate a glad awareness of your God-given personality and then a desire to use the particular gifts of your personality type for the love of God and the service of others.

You then have to uncover the hidden gifts of your personality that do not come so easily or naturally to you, but which are the source of new growth, great enjoyment and childlike trust. That requires ruthless honesty with yourself, tempered by an invincible conviction of God's unconditional love for you. Finally, you must give yourself the space and light you need to grow by weeding out all that is deceitful, hypocritical, and unworthy of God's gift of life, all your foolish self-interest, ambition, false humility, fear, cowardice and hostility. The continual labour to shed the immature, false and egotistical self is our part in putting on Christ.

It is easy to give lip-service to all that, but very difficult to do it. Just accepting your gifts of personality and being glad to be you is hard enough, but turning to face the Shadow in yourself and then dealing with what it brings to light requires considerable courage.

Becoming what God has in mind for you to be is a process of 'being changed into his likeness from one degree of glory to another'. The more you become your true self, through prayer 'beholding the glory of the Lord', the more Christlike you become. Paul, who knew all about the need for discipline in the Christian life, insisted that ultimately our Christification is not our doing but 'comes from the Lord who is the Spirit'.[9] 'I am quite certain that the One who began this good work in you will see that it is finished when the Day of Christ Jesus comes.'[10]

## Prayer and Type Development

Growth in psychological maturity goes hand in hand with growth in your understanding of God. Both lead to new opportunities for your prayer-relationship. Often, however, those opportunities appear at first as problems in prayer.

Personality is a seed, sown by God, that develops by slow stages throughout life. Personality type is dynamic not static, a process, not a diagnosis. Your 'true type' is inborn, but it will develop throughout your life. By God's grace you will reveal it, grow into it, and gradually become the person you have it in you to be. That personal development includes physical, emotional, mental, social and spiritual growth, each of which have their own staging posts.

## Childhood

Roughly speaking, up to about six years of age the four functions of the personality are not clearly differentiated. Watch a small child for an hour or two and you will see her or him trying out each function in turn, in extraverted ways and in introverted ways. At one moment the child is perceiving in an extraverted sensing way, gazing intently at a beetle, taking in every detail, completely present in the moment. Not long afterwards that child is caught up in introverted intuitive perception, playing a long, imaginative and solitary game. When the sweets are handed round, the child can be seen entering the realms of thinking judgement, insisting on just and logical criteria for the fair distribution of the goodies. Then feeling judgement takes over as that same child tries to please and to make everyone happy.

Small children have a natural religious sense and a remarkable ability to detect humbug in adults. Teaching little children to 'say their prayers' is a hazardous enterprise, as is teaching them about God. I am not suggesting that we should not teach children to pray, merely that our well-meaning efforts can so easily hinder a genuine openness to faith. The Christian faith, after all, is more like measles than spelling: it is caught, not taught. In the earliest years of life a child will imbibe it from the love, security and example of parents and family.

From about the age of six to adolescence a child, given the chance, will manifest one of the four functions, in either an extraverted or an introverted way, as the dominant function of the personality. If you think back to your own childhood it is quite likely that you will be able to identify your emerging dominant function in your behaviour and relationships. I can remember my dominant introverted intuitive function making itself clearly felt in primary school. I was a loner and lived much of the time in a world of fantasy and imagination, working things out in my mind and often out of touch with external reality. That is how I describe it. My extraverted sensing teachers had a different view and saw me as unsociable, lacking in attention and under-achieving.

That first function to be clearly differentiated, your dominant, will be the one throughout life to which you turn most naturally and easily in conscious prayer.

## Adolescence

From puberty to about the age of twenty, the auxiliary function usually appears. As a rule, if your dominant function is extraverted your auxiliary will be introverted; if your dominant is an introverted function, your auxiliary will be extraverted.

This psychological development combined with the physiological changes of adolescence can create a potent, exciting and sometimes distressing mix. The adolescent is often operating out of his or her second-best function. The child who had been so extravert will become withdrawn and moody, while the introverted one will become noisy and outgoing.

I can remember how in my own adolescence the newly emerging auxiliary function, in my case extraverted feeling, opened up wonderful new horizons in my life. It drew me out to the world of friendships, the local youth club, amateur dramatics, and the desire to change the world into a happier place.

Prayer in the auxiliary function of your personality may have played a noticeably important part at that stage of your life. However, in dynamic partnership with your dominant, it forms a powerful combination for your spiritual formation throughout the whole of your life.

## Early Adulthood

Young adulthood, the years from twenty to thirty-five or so, is often a time of consolidation of the dominant and auxiliary functions of the personality. It is also very often the time when the tertiary function emerges and is appreciated. As an INFJ type, my tertiary function is thinking judgement, and I can recognise how in my twenties and thirties that logical and analytical process came into play as I was drawn to academic, organisational and administrative work.

Meeting God in prayer through the tertiary function will often be attractive and fruitful for the young adult.

The first half of life tends to be more active. You feel that you are seeking God, trying to discover and understand God. You are taking action, making decisions, undertaking responsibilities, perhaps laying the foundation of a career or a family. You are busy, using mainly your dominant and auxiliary functions, but also the tertiary. If conditions for you have been ideal, which they rarely are, your prayer relationship is likely to focus through the dominant function, where you feel comfortable, skilful and in control. However, it will also include aspects of your auxiliary and tertiary functions.

## Mid-Life

It is as you enter the second half of life that things begin to change, often in a disturbing and disruptive way. The notorious mid-life crisis is a turning point. It is the time when you face uncomfortable truths about yourself and your life.

Perhaps you have not become the person you wanted to be or, worse, you are becoming the person you certainly did not want to be. Possibly the children are leaving home and you wish you had been a better parent. Maybe your marriage relationship has become tired and routine. You yearn for love and new zest in life as you look back longingly at the optimism and fun of your youth. You feel trapped in a way of life or an occupation that is life-denying rather than life-fulfilling. Yet it is too late to start again. The range of options for your life has become increasingly limited. It is a time of wishing you had, and regretting you did not.

At the same time, mid-life unfurls for you new possibilities. Somehow it is now easier to be yourself with new courage and confidence, without having to worry about what other people think. You glimpse in yourself exciting and challenging hidden potential. There is an urge towards wholeness, ripeness and a new affirming of your distinctive being.

At a dinner party a Jewish friend was pulling my leg about the attitude of some Christians to the mid-life crisis. 'You Anglicans', he said, 'seem to think that life begins at birth. Catholics say that life begins at conception. But we Jews know that life really begins when the dog dies and the children leave home!'

## The Second Half of Life

The second half of life is therefore a time of new beginnings. There is an urge for integration. As you thank God for your talents, you ask for help to become the best that you can be.

You now become increasingly aware of the gift that God has given to you in your fourth, inferior function. Up to now it may well have been troublesome, manifesting itself in more negative than positive ways. You may have come to know it through your behaviour when you are 'out of control', 'not yourself'. The inferior function, as you have seen, can erupt unbidden into consciousness when you are tired, stressed or angry, bringing up with it some of the contents of our unconscious Shadow personality.

As the opposite to your dominant, the inferior function has been a neglected part of your personality but now in mid-life it cries out for attention, urging you towards a new discovery of the Self. Increasingly in your prayer relationship you turn to the opposite 'colour' to your dominant, because it is there that the ego has least control. In that weak, immature, habitually neglected area of personality God finds your Achilles heel, which is another way of saying that God comes to you not so much in your strength as in your weakness. 'For it is when I am weak that I am strong.'[11]

The second half of life is a time for learning about your Shadow, and for discovering that God is there too, loving you into new integrity of being. It is a time for learning to stop trying so hard, to be more passive, and more and more to trust in the Lord who says, 'My grace is enough for you: my power is at its best in weakness.'[12] So gradually, as you grow older, you learn to relinquish self-control in favour of God-control.

In middle age and onwards you want to be rather than to do. You are more willing to flout convention when it conflicts with your personal integrity, more able to face life with high-hearted happiness. As Jung put it, 'In every adult there lurks a child – an eternal child, something that is always becoming, is never completed, and calls for unceasing care, attention, and education. That is the part of the human personality which wants to develop and become whole.'[13]

For many, mid- and later-life is a period of new conversion, of an even more trustful and confident turning to face God as you learn to face yourself with greater honesty, understanding and love. Head knowledge or heart knowledge now becomes 'head-and-heart' faith in the God and Father of our Lord Jesus Christ.

In the second half of life there comes a new realisation that with God there are no recriminations, simply superabundant joy that you have come to your senses and turned back to him. 'While he was still a long way off, his father saw him and was moved with pity. He ran to the boy, clasped him in his arms and kissed him tenderly.'[14]

Many people for whom prayer has been a burdensome duty make the liberating discovery, in the second half of life, that prayer is not something that you have to make time for, but the way you live life. They echo P.T. Forsyth's words, 'We pray because we are made for prayer, and God draws us out by breathing himself in.'

Of course there is nothing inevitable about any of this. You can abuse God's gift of free will by denying the law of your own being. You can renounce your wholeness and submit to self-pity, pride, bitterness of spirit, complaining and many other unattractive traits displayed by some elderly people.

'True personality,' Jung said, 'is always a vocation and puts its trust in God.'[15] You are *called* to be you, and the 'you' you are called to be is in every sense lovely. As with any vocation from God, it does not just happen but you have to make a deliberate, conscious response. 'That is the great and liberating thing about any genuine personality: he voluntarily sacrifices himself to his vocation.'[16]

For many people, prayer in the second half of life is far less anxious and active. There is a greater awareness of God's nearness. 'The nearer you go to God, the nearer he will come to you.'[17] Extraverts and introverts alike report a movement towards more silence in prayer, more listening and waiting on God. In retrospect you can see how God has loved and guided you along the way and answered your unconscious prayers rather than giving you what you thought you wanted.

> I asked for strength that I might achieve.
> He made me weak that I might obey.
> I asked for health that I might do great things.
> I was given grace that I might do better things.
> I asked for riches that I might be happy.
> I was given poverty that I might be wise.
> I asked for power that I might have the praise of men.
> I was given weakness that I might feel the need for God.
> I asked for all things that I might enjoy life.

I was given life that I might enjoy all things.
I received nothing that I asked for,
All that I hoped for.
My prayer was answered.[18]

# Holistic Prayer

## The Archetype of Order

As Angelo Spoto has pointed out,[1] in using the Myers-Briggs typology we can all too easily get caught up in the archetype of order which would have us classify personality types in clear 'black and white' ways. Everything about human personality and the differences between people has to be made to fit the theory. 'The more its audience needs to have everything fit in a neat and orderly way', Spoto writes, 'the more Jung's work becomes rigid and ossified.' The Myers-Briggs typology, if incompletely understood and inexpertly applied, can lead us into the temptation to stereotype people and to be altogether too cut, dried and predictive about personality types.

When using type theory we must always remember that there are many other things that affect who we are and how we behave. Our religious faith, our motivations and anxieties, our social, cultural and educational background, our intelligence, age, gender and sexual orientation – these and many other factors add to the richness of personality differences. Jung himself remarked that every individual is an exception to the rule, so that 'one can never give a description of a type, no matter how complete, that would apply to more than one individual, despite the fact that in some ways it aptly characterises thousands of others. Conformity is one side of man, uniqueness is the other. Classification does not explain the individual psyche.'[2]

## Colourful Personalities

Within each type, therefore, there are as many variations as there are people of that type, and they are all lovely expressions of the image of God. For that reason, as a deliberate attempt to blur the edges of type and prayer classifications, I have come to think of the sixteen Myers-Briggs types in terms of colour.[3] A favourite visual aid to illustrate that analogy in my workshops is a large sampler card of dozens of different coloured needlepoint wool. The difference between, say, green wool and red wool is comparable to the difference between, say, an ESTP person and an ENFJ person. We can think of ESTP personalities clustering on the green part of the colour spectrum and the ENFJs sitting on the red part of the rainbow.

On my sampler card each colour has very many different shades. Among the reds, for instance, you will find everything from pale pink to scarlet, and the colours have evocative names such as spice, bittersweet, tangerine, rusty rose, hot pink, American beauty, ginger, Christmas red, strawberry and cranberry. Furthermore, each one of those shades of red has a variety of different hues.

If you think of personality type in those colour terms you will avoid the temptation to have 'everything fit in a neat and orderly way'. You will see that people who share the same Myers-Briggs type do not all necessarily prefer to pray in the same way. You will see that you can never be a clone of others of your type. While it is true that all ESTP personalities have certain characteristics in common, it is also true that no ESTP is like any other ESTP. One is lime green, another is emerald, and a third is an earthy green. One ENFJ person is a jolly tomato red, another is a dull crimson, and a third is shocking pink. Each person is in God's eyes unique, precious, beautiful and infinitely loved. Every individual is a reflection of the beauty and Person of God, a unique manifestation of God's love in creation.

Colours owe their existence to light, just as personalities owe their existence to God. What you see as a lovely colour is a complex mixture of various visible wavelengths of light. Colours are a combination of hue, tone and intensity, none of which is visible in isolation. You change a colour's hue by adding another colour to it. You change its tone, making it darker or lighter, by shading it with black or tinting it with white. The brilliance or intensity depends on the amount of pure colour in the mix.

Colours influence our emotions, and colour preference is a very personal matter. Max Lüscher based his analysis of personality on individual colour preferences which, he claimed, show individuality almost as precisely as a fingerprint.

In colour terms, God is pure white light. Pure white is the

colour of goodness and holiness. Pure black, the negation of colour, often means death and mourning. It can be a symbol of evil (which makes me wonder why the colour traditionally worn by clergy is black and not white!). However, shades of black are often very beautiful, as for instance in human skin colour. The darkness of the Shadow and of what St John of the Cross called the Dark Night of the Soul, is not malevolent but a source of strength and power.

The Religious Society of Friends, known as the Quakers, describe themselves as 'a prism through which the Divine Light passes to become visible in a spectrum of many colours; many more in their richness than words alone can express'.

That analogy can be applied to all humanity. As the Friends teach, there is 'that of God in everyone'. The life of God is the light of humanity, 'a light that shines in the dark, a light that darkness could not overpower'.[4] 'The true light that enlightens all men'[5] is the creative Word of God made flesh in Jesus Christ.

The human race then, created in God's image, is a prism through which the light of God refracts into the colours of our individual personalities.

## Colour and the Four Functions

God gives to you, his beloved child, a coat of many colours that you wear by using your personality to the full. There is a lovely connection that Jung noticed between colour and the four functions, S, N, T and F.[6] He discovered that fourfold symbols often occur in dreams as the four principal colours, red, blue, green and yellow. 'It happens with some regularity', he wrote, 'that these colours are correlated with the four orienting functions of consciousness.'[7]

Green, the colour of nature, is the Sensing colour. Sunny, inspirational yellow is the colour for Intuition. The cool, calm blue of sky and ocean, noble and lofty, is the colour for the Thinking function. The warm and joyful reds link well with Feeling judgement. To the points of Jung's compass, therefore, we can add the corresponding colours:

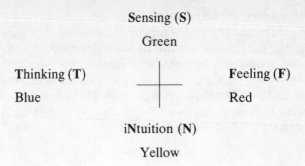

Sensing (S)
Green

Thinking (T)                                        Feeling (F)
Blue                                                Red

iNtuition (N)
Yellow

## Green for Sensing

Green is the colour of life itself, the colour of the environment, of foliage, of spring. It is the most natural and restful colour. It focuses almost exactly on the retina, and so is the most peaceful colour to the eye. To ease their eyes from the strain of close work, engravers used to keep a green beryl handy, to look at from time to time.

Green is a sensible and emotionally balanced colour, giving a sense of stability and security. It is not intrusive or dominating, and so is used for surgeons' gowns, snooker tables and the green baize doors leading to the servants' quarters in grand houses. It symbolises faithfulness, gladness and victory. Green is the liturgical colour used for vestments and hangings in church throughout the long 'growing' season between Pentecost and Advent.

All colours have their negative side, and green is no exception. For some people green is a poisonous colour, associated with envy, jealousy and nausea. However, the green that makes one person feel nauseous will seem bright and refreshing to another.

## Yellow for Intuition

Yellow, like the well differentiated intuitive function, is happy and optimistic. It is bright and cheerful, the colour of gold, of sunlight and of children's toys. It reminds us of spring flowers, daffodils, crocuses, primroses, forsythia, winter jasmine, and of the lovely yellow-brown tints of autumn.

Yellow radiates warmth and inspiration, and is the most reflective of all colours. Buddhist monks wear robes of saffron yellow. Cloth of gold is used liturgically for great festivals of the Church.

Just as the gift of intuition can be misunderstood, feared, and abused, so yellow can be seen as a fearful, liverish, heretical colour. It is sometimes associated with cowardice and betrayal. In medieval art Judas Iscariot is often portrayed in yellow robes. The Nazis made Jews wear yellow armbands, and in France the doors of traitors were daubed with yellow paint.

## Blue for Thinking

The thinking colour conjures up images of vast expanses of sky and ocean, loftiness and depth, nobility and rationality. It points to the depths of the intellect and to the heights of heaven. The shades on my sampler card have such names as Blue Spruce, Glacier and Caribbean Blue. Blue, like the mature Thinking function, is cool, restful, and spacious. Blue surroundings have a soothing and calming effect.

Blue can mean the best, as in blue-blood and blue-stocking, and the highest office or honour as in the Blue Ribbon of the Garter or, applied to the Archbishopric of Canterbury, of the Church of England. It symbolises prudence, a good conscience, sincerity and loyalty to the faith of Christ. The Scottish Presbyterian Covenantors wore blue to remind themselves of the children of Israel who in Numbers 15:38 were commanded to decorate their garments with blue tassels. Liturgically it is rarely used except in Spain, occasionally, for festivals of the Blessed Virgin Mary.

Blue does have its negative side too, mainly seamy and melancholic. We talk about indecent films as blue movies, and the blue pencil of censorship. We describe depression as feeling blue, and the slaves of the American Deep South expressed their unhappiness by singing the blues. However, the negative side of blue is never threatening, and it has a curious self-righting property. Blue skies lift depression. Singing blues gives pleasure and relief.

## Red for Feeling

Red, with the longest wavelength and lowest energy of all visible light, sits at the top of the rainbow. Of all the colours, the reds have the greatest emotional impact. The Feeling function is the colour of the heart, the natural colour of blood and of fire, a dynamic, vibrant and restless colour. It demands attention and radiates warmth.

Red is the colour of joy and revelry, red wine, painting the town red, a red-letter day. Pink is more gentle and feminine, blooming with health and happiness. When we are not off-colour, we feel in the pink, and everything is rosy. When our emotions are touched, we blush, and when we are angry we go red in the face.

In Church liturgy red is traditionally associated with Christian love and is used for festivals of the Holy Spirit and of martyrs.

The negative meanings of the feeling colour can be quite frightening. Red is the colour of danger, aggression and lust. A red rag to a bull excites rage. A red light district is the haunt of prostitutes. The scarlet woman of St John's vision is the mother of harlots and abominations, identified with the Church of Rome by Protestant bigots and with the Protestant churches by Catholic bigots.

## Holistic Prayer

The peacock, with its gloriously colourful tail, is a traditional symbol of the resurrection. 'All I want', wrote Paul, 'is to know Christ and the power of his resurrection.'[8] That desire to know Christ, to share his resurrection life and grow into his likeness, underlies all our desire for prayer. A faithful prayer-relationship gradually integrates the many colours of our personality into a single colour, God's colour, white.

We are familiar with the idea of holistic medicine, which aims to treat the whole person rather than merely the diseased parts of the body or mind. In a similar way my notion of holistic prayer is a reminder that true prayer is being your whole self before the holy God. Holistic prayer is the whole personality, conscious and unconscious, worshipping the Triune God. Like Aaron's robe and Christ's robe, the robe of prayer is a one-piece garment that must not be torn or divided.

It is all too easy to latch on to the idea that if you are, say, an –S–P type then it will follow, as night follows day, that the Franciscan tradition of spirituality will attract you, and that –S–J types will undoubtedly benefit from the Ignatian exercises. However, working with many hundreds of people in prayer and spirituality workshops has shown me that the connection between personality type and prayer is not that simple or predictable.

Your psychological type does inevitably colour your experience of God, but it neither offers a set menu for your prayer life nor implies a self-indulgent 'smorgasbord spirituality' for you to select attractive bits from here and there and discard the rest. On the contrary, enrichment of your prayer relationship by understanding your own personality type comes about by a genuine synthesis of all the ways of prayer suggested by the various gifts of personality. Whatever your type may be, in a fully rounded prayer-relationship the four functions of the psyche, dominant, auxiliary, tertiary and inferior, will work together as a dynamic whole.

## Awareness and Response

A holistic prayer life is a continual rhythm, breathing in *awareness* of God, and breathing out *response* to God.

Awareness corresponds to the perceiving functions, S and N. You open your heart and mind to become aware of God with the meditative and contemplative forms of prayer, with green prayer, which is sensing, and yellow prayer, which is intuitive.

Response corresponds to the judging functions, T and F. In the prayer of response you take action before God in intercession, petition, confession, thanksgiving, and all the active forms of prayer. This is the blue prayer of the thinking function, and the red prayer of your psyche's feeling function.

## The Christian Heritage

Christians have a gloriously rich legacy of spirituality. Great women and men of prayer have passed on to us their experience and advice, people as varied as Dietrich Bonhoeffer, Anthony of the Desert, Julian of Norwich, Evelyn Underhill, Thomas à Kempis, Basil of Caesarea, Teresa of Avila. Linked to the names of great spiritual leaders are the many different traditions of spirituality, Benedictine, Franciscan, Ignatian, Lutheran, and so on. Some schools of prayer have denominational roots, such as Anglican, Catholic, Orthodox and Wesleyan, while others spring from a particular cultural or political milieu, notably the Celtic, Feminist, Black and Liberation spiritualities.

These many different strands in our Christian heritage are there to be discovered, cherished and used by all believers. Unfortunately many Christians are ignorant of any paths of prayer beyond those handed down to them through the filter of their own denominational emphases.

That situation is gradually changing as a more tolerant ecumenical climate encourages Christians to cross denominational boundaries and open themselves to the insights, wisdom and practices of unfamiliar ways of prayer. As we increasingly value the diverse contributions of different personality types, we will give greater understanding and respect to the rich diversity and mutual interdependence in prayer within the single body of Christ.

## Image-filled and Imageless Prayer

The Christian spiritual tradition contains pairs of opposing strands that match the opposing poles of personality functions. One such pair is the cataphatic tradition and the apophatic tradition. They correspond to ways of prayer through the perceiving functions of S and N respectively.

Cataphatic prayer has to do with what we can know about God. It is image-filled, specific, affirmative, historical, and incarnational. The cataphatic way celebrates the immanent God, manifested in creation, sacrament and Scripture.

Apophatic prayer, on the other hand, points to the unknowability of God. It reminds us that before God we are reduced to silent awe in the Cloud of Unknowing. It is the prayer of mystical, imageless contemplation. The apophatic way is a self-emptying union with the transcendent and ultimately nameless God.

Holistic Christian prayer must not choose between the apophatic and the cataphatic way, though by the nature of your personality one will attract you more than the other. Rather, you must delight in both, living with the resulting paradox and creative tension until you discover true synthesis, a new consciousness that is both apophatic and cataphatic. Thomas Merton described that new form of consciousness as

a totally different kind of self-awareness from that of the Cartesian thinking-self which is its own justification and its own center. Here the individual is aware of himself as a self-to-be-dissolved in self-giving, in love, in letting-go, in ecstasy, in God – there are many ways of phrasing it. It does not consider God either as immanent or transcendent but as grace and presence, hence neither as a 'Center' imagined somewhere 'out there' nor 'within ourselves'. It encounters Him not as Being but as Freedom and Love.⁹

## Prayer of the Mind and of the Heart

Another pair of opposing strands in the Christian spiritual tradition is the speculative and affective ways of prayer, matching the judging functions of T and F respectively. Holistic prayer also demands a real synthesis between those opposite ways of prayer.

The speculative way emphasises the rational and intellectual approach to God. That will usually have a special appeal for thinking types, whereas feeling types may warm more to the affective ways of prayer that focus on the emotions. True holistic prayer is not either speculative or affective, but both. 'Surely', Paul wrote, 'I should pray not only with the spirit but with the mind as well?'¹⁰

It may be, as Martin Thornton suggested, that the synthesis of head and heart, the welding of 'true piety and sound learning', is the deepest meaning of the Anglican *via media*.

> The affective-speculative synthesis does not mean an exact fifty-fifty balance. It is a synthesis, not merely a mixture, and the true synthesis is possible to different temperaments. Everyone has a natural bias to one side or the other, and spiritual health is attained by allowing this bias to be permeated by the other aspect through mental and emotional discipline.¹¹

Dame Julian of Norwich and an eleventh-century Archbishop of Canterbury, St Anselm, were both outstanding examples of spiritual speculative-affective harmony. In her *Revelations of Divine Love*, Julian of Norwich 'combines the most vivid, most disturbing affective meditation on every distressing detail of the Passion with almost a treatise on the doctrine of the Atonement.'¹²

Holistic prayer is ever-increasing consciousness of our corporate relatedness to and dependence on the one true God who loves us more than we can ever imagine, and who desires to give us, moment by moment, more than we can ever desire or deserve. Methods, techniques and traditions of prayer have value only if they draw us more closely to God. They are there to help us towards what an English Cistercian monk, William of St Thierry, described as 'the perpetual mindfulness of God, the continual striving of the will to the understanding of him, the unwearied affection to the loving of him.'[13]

In holistic prayer there is, as the Preacher said, a time for everything. There is a time for quiet awareness of God with all our senses, a time for intuitive dreaming, a time for thinking and reading, and a time for loving and being loved. For everyone there is an important time, too, for coming to God through our less preferred functions and attitudes. Then the weak and immature child in us can come out to laugh and play – and to pray.

> Take time to think –
> It is the source of power.
> Take time to read –
> It is the foundation of wisdom.
> Take time to play –
> It is the secret of staying young.
> Take time to be quiet –
> It is the opportunity to seek God.
>
> Take time to be aware –
> It is the opportunity to help others.
> Take time to love and be loved –
> It is God's greatest gift.
>
> Take time to laugh –
> It is the music of the soul.
> Take time to be friendly –
> It is the road to happiness.
>
> Take time to dream –
> It is what the future is made of.
> Take time to pray –
> It is the greatest power on earth.

## Four as a Symbol of Wholeness

The number four is a common and powerful symbol of wholeness and individuation. For instance, in Christian iconography it is usually only Jesus who has a halo divided into four parts, symbolising his perfection. We speak of the four corners of the world, meaning the whole world. Among many other examples of quaternity symbolising wholeness are the four animals in Ezekiel's vision, the four animals of Revelation, the four Evangelists, the quarters of a city, the four arms of the Cross, and the heavenly Jerusalem with three times four gates and God as its centre.

The four functions of Jung's model of personality may also be seen as symbolising wholeness. To these functions with their related colours we can now add the perceiving and judging polarities of Christian spiritual traditions:

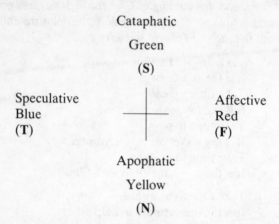

Cataphatic

Green

(**S**)

Speculative          Affective
Blue                 Red
(**T**)              (**F**)

Apophatic

Yellow

(**N**)

Holistic prayer embraces the four functions in both the extraverted and the introverted attitude. The green prayer of the sensing function, for instance, focuses either on the specific realities of the outer world or on internal, mental sensory impressions. That distinction between extraverted sensing and introverted sensing is important and applies equally to the yellow prayer of intuition, the blue prayer of thinking and the red prayer of the feeling function.

## Extravert Prayer

Prayer for the extravert-preferring person is not simply or primarily an inward journey. An ENFP woman described it to me as, 'Living your life alongside God. You don't go inside yourself to pray. It is what you are doing and what you are saying. Things hit you from the world, and you say, "Thank you, God", or "Please help me", or "Why me?" '

Extraverted spirituality is often 'prayer in action', practical acts of love and compassion. Your work can be your prayer. I was reminded of this throughout my training at theological college, as we passed daily through the library to reach the chapel. Over the entrance to the chapel was written 'Orare est Labore', prayer is work; and over the door on the way out from the chapel, back to the library, was written 'Labore est Orare', work is prayer.

Extravert types, as we have seen, will often work things out as they talk. They reach their best insights through talking, and that is often true also in their prayer. Sharing with others in prayer is important for extraverts, and their perceiving and judging preferences will draw them to the types of personalities they find it easy to share with.

Extraverts have often told me that they are made to feel guilty by introverted types because they have difficulty finding God within themselves. Spiritual writers urge them to pray silently and give the impression that the silent inward journey is, if not the only way of prayer, certainly the best way. 'Listen to Him and talk with Him, not with the lips, but in the heart', a holy saint tells us. Extraverts may struggle valiantly to do that, and wonder why they find it so very difficult when others around them seem to find it comparatively easy and natural.

I strongly suspect that most people who write and teach about prayer are introverts, probably introverted intuitives. They must beware of assuming that their preferred and natural way of relating to God must be the right way for everyone. They live in the inner world by preference. Extraverts, however, live in the outer world. That is where they are most at home. They naturally relate to people and things, and are usually good conversationalists. They enjoy small talk. All these preferences will be reflected in their natural way of praying.

## Prayer in Action

For them, the prayer relationship is never divorced from immediate, practical action. I like to think that in the parable of the Good Samaritan the priest and the Levite who passed by on the other side were introverted types. When they had gone a mile or so further down the road, they came to the conclusion that they should have helped the man in the ditch but by then it was too late. The immediate, spontaneous practical act of love and pity by the Samaritan traveller was a typical extraverted response. More precisely, it was an extraverted sensing and feeling response such as ESFP types, who are always excellent in crisis situations, might give.

It really is not helpful or accurate for introverts to say, 'Ah, but helping someone isn't *really* prayer'. For extraverts such practical acts of compassion really *are* prayer and they need to be told so.

## Extraverts and the Church

The unrelieved introverted intuitive ethos of much that goes on in the institutional Church is quite contrary to the active, hands-on, fun-loving style so characteristic of many extraverts, particularly the ESFP and ESTP types. Try asking a group of ES–P people to give their immediate associations to the word 'church'. Responses such as 'boring', 'dull' and 'uninteresting' will appear too often for the comfort of church members, and especially those of us in positions of church leadership.

Surely, we think, if they really understood what liturgy is about they would be as absorbed by it as we are. If they could only grasp the real meaning of fellowship they would find it as enjoyable and fulfilling as we do. If only they could be like us the churches would be full!

Most ES–P types enjoy practical demonstrations rather than ideas. They want to see things happen. They prefer to learn by doing, as any teacher knows. 'I hear and I forget. I see and I remember. I do and I learn.' When their worship is practical, lively and active it becomes interesting, exciting and quite the opposite of boring.

Although 35–40 per cent of the population are –S–P types, the adaptable realists in society, very few of them are members of mainline church congregations. Less than 5 per cent of ordained ministers in the Church of England are –S–P types.[14] In the present Decade of Evangelism that fact deserves to be treated with the utmost seriousness.

## Introverted Prayer

Introverts focus their energy and attention on the inner world of thought and reflection, and so their natural inclination in prayer will be to withdraw to discover God within themselves. They need reflective time alone with God in a way that extraverts do not. That is not to say that extraverts have no ability or desire to embark on the inward journey of prayer. Extraverts need to introvert, just as introverts need to extravert. Nevertheless, if you are an extravert your primary focus will be outwards, and if you are an introvert your primary focus will be inwards. That preferred focus is your individual gift and always takes priority, in prayer as in any other aspect of life.

# The Perceiving Functions: Passive Prayer

Green prayer and yellow prayer together encompass the human way of experiencing God. They are the prayer of simply knowing God, rather than knowing or thinking *about* God. They are a conversion of attention towards God.

Through them you open yourself to conscious awareness of the Divine and you attend to God. Green and yellow prayer are passive, receptive and contemplative ways of praying, but one is clearly focused on inner and outer realities while the other is unfocused, dreamy and abstracted.

*Sensing Prayer*

### Green Prayer – The Sensing Gift

| Dominant Sensing | Auxiliary Sensing | Tertiary Sensing | Inferior Sensing |
|---|---|---|---|
| ESFP | ESFJ | ENFJ | ENFP |
| ESTP | ESTJ | ENTJ | ENTP |
| ISFJ | ISFP | INFP | INFJ |
| ISTJ | ISTP | INTP | INTJ |

If S is dominant or auxiliary in your type, you will probably find green prayer is the way you most naturally relate to God.

If S is your tertiary or inferior, the sensing function can be unpredictable and unruly. You therefore need to get in touch with it in a positive, deliberate, playful and prayerful way. You may benefit from giving special attention to green prayer, particularly in the second half of life when you will probably find that you are increasingly drawn to it anyway.

So what is green prayer? For me, it is summed up in this poem by
e.e. cummings:[1]

> i thank You God for most this amazing
> day:for the leaping greenly spirits of trees
> and a blue true dream of sky;and for everything
> which is natural which is infinite which is yes
>
> (i who have died am alive again today,
> and this is the sun's birthday;this is the birth
> day of life and of love and wings:and of the gay
> great happening illimitably earth)
>
> how should tasting touching hearing seeing
> breathing any—lifted from the no
> of all nothing—human merely being
> doubt unimaginable You?
>
> (now the ears of my ears awake and
> now the eyes of my eyes are opened)

In green prayer you are looking and listening with awakened ears
and opened eyes, the eyes and ears of faith. You are simply there,
attending to God with faith and reverence. Abstract ideas and
theological arguments fade away as you meet the Creator through
the reality of creation.

> not
> all matterings of mind
> equal one violet[2]

You discover God in whatever gives you joy or pain, and in whatever disturbs or excites you. You find God in and through everything. You see how all creation manifests God, sings to God,
praises God, and gives joy to God. 'Sing to Yahweh, all the earth!
. . . let earth rejoice . . . let the fields exult and all that is in
them, let all the woodland trees cry out for joy, at the presence
of Yahweh.'[3] The universe, and our small world in it, and the
infinitesimal speck of creation that is you, are the visible outpouring of God's exultant love. 'May Yahweh find joy in what he
creates!'[4]

Your five senses give you the ability to perceive directly, clearly
and accurately. In green prayer you are paying attention to God in
the alert and clearly focused way that comes naturally to dominant
S types, and is less easy but hugely worthwhile for the rest of us.

That focused attention in green prayer may be extraverted or introverted. Either way, it has a particular quality that always reminds me of my little Jack Russell dog. She loved nothing better than to chase a ball. When I picked up a ball to throw, nothing else in the world mattered to her. Her eyes never strayed from it for one instant. Her whole being was focused on that ball with a concentration of unwavering attention. That is the way of attending to God that I think of as green prayer: rapt, eager, expectant, happy.

Every sensory perception is a doorway to God. Open that door, and you are like the man who had been born blind and whose answer to the sceptics was, 'I only know that I was blind and now I can see.'[5] In the *Way of a Pilgrim* that green prayer experience is beautifully described:

> Everything around me became transformed and I saw it in a new and delightful way. The trees, the grass, the earth, the air, the light, and everything seemed to be saying to me that it exists to witness to God's love and that it prays and sings of God's glory. . . I saw how it was possible to communicate with God's creation.[6]

When we lived in Devon my wife and I loved to walk on Exmoor and Dartmoor. In the wide open silent space of the moorlands, with the feel of the springy turf under our feet, our souls could quieten and then expand.

> It was like a church to me,
> I entered it on soft foot,
> Breath held like a cap in the hand.
> It was quiet.
> What God was there made himself felt,
> Not listened to, in clean colours
> That brought a moistening of the eye,
> In movement of the wind over grass.

> There were no prayers said. But stillness
> Of the heart's passions – that was praise
> Enough; and the mind's cession
> Of its kingdom. I walked on,
> Simple and poor, while the air crumbled
> And broke on me generously as bread.[7]

Green prayer is receptive, meditative and contemplative. It is the prayer of directly being with God and patiently waiting on God, like the old man who used to sit in church for hours on end. Noticing that he was not saying any prayers or telling his beads, the parish priest became curious and asked him one day, 'What are you doing all the time, when you sit in the church every day?' 'Well,' replied the old man, 'I just sit and I look. I look at Him and He looks at me.' That is simple, contemplative and, in my terms, green prayer.

By cultivating green prayer you can counterbalance the activism of Western civilisation. 'Sitting quietly, doing nothing, spring comes and the grass grows by itself.'[8] For Christians, sitting quietly with God, doing nothing, is not a waste of time. Sometimes you need to bring into consciousness the promise of our Risen Lord that he will be with you always, to the end of time. You can then bask in simple awareness of the Lord's presence, just spending time in his company.

## Finding God in All Things

Meister Eckhart, one of the fourteenth-century Rhineland mystics, said that it is only because of our imperfection that we have a special awareness of God in quiet or beautiful places, in the fields or in church. In truth, God can be found as much in noise as in silence, in squalor as in beauty, for 'God is equally in all things and all places, and is equally ready to give Himself as far as in Him lies. . . God is closer to me than I am to myself.'[9]

The seventeenth-century monk, Brother Lawrence of the Resurrection, took up the same theme in his little book *The Practice of the Presence of God*. 'The time of business does not with me differ from the time of prayer; and in the noise and clatter of my kitchen, while several persons are at the same time calling for different things, I possess God in as great tranquillity as if I were upon my knees at the blessed sacrament.'[10]

## Cataphatic Prayer

I said earlier that green prayer is cataphatic, filled with positive images of the God of history. You know from experience that the God of your own tiny personal history is trustworthy. His hand has always been upon you. You are sure that God, your Father, your

Mother, who has been so good and faithful to you in the past, will be good and faithful to you now and always. All your senses speak to you of God's goodness, wisdom and love. The gospel is not about fairy-tales or fantasies, but about God made known in the historical Jesus. It is about realities, the real God come to earth as a real Human Person to open the door to real life, eternal life.

> Something which has existed since the beginning,
> that we have heard,
> and we have seen with our own eyes;
> that we have watched
> and touched with our hands:
> the Word, who is life –
> this is our subject.
> That life was made visible:
> we saw it and we are giving our testimony,
> telling you of the eternal life
> which was with the Father and has been made visible to us.[11]

### Incarnational Prayer

Green prayer is, above all, incarnational prayer. The royal road to redemption and new life, blazed by Christ, was not other-worldly, rose-strewn and painless, but the Way of the Cross. Green prayer makes it impossible for you to float through life with an unreal, romantic view of Christian discipleship. It constantly brings you down-to-earth to see God present in all the commonplace realities of life, particularly in ugliness, degradation, pain and poverty. Christians have sometimes tried to exclude God from great tracts of reality that they have labelled 'profane', or 'secular', or even 'natural'. Through green prayer the Holy Spirit arouses us to ever greater awareness of God in all things and in all events, however tragic, disgusting or banal.

### Restful and Grateful Prayer

There is an ease of perception about shades of green. In a theatre the peaceful back stage sanctuary, a calming, soothing place for the actors, is the Green Room. Green prayer has a similar effect.

It is easy, natural and restful, quieting jangled nerves, stilling your mind, and leaving you feeling refreshed.

It is prayer of the body. Sitting, kneeling, standing; hands together, open to receive, or lifted in praise; relaxing, listening, looking – what you do with your body is very important for sensing prayer. You may be one of the many people who prefer to pray while walking. People talking to me about their prayer have often said that it is their pet dog, more than anything else, who ensures their regular daily prayer times!

Sensing prayer is prayer full of praise and gratitude. Goethe claimed that the eye experiences 'a distinctly grateful impression' from the colour green. In green prayer you are constantly wanting to give thanks and praise to God for sights and sounds and smells, for the taste and the feel of things, for the beauty of creation, lovely flowers, food, creatures, music, works of art. The arthritic hands of an old lady at the Communion rail, the whiff of an autumn bonfire, a good wine, a hot bath after a hard day, the sound of a village band at a Maltese *festa* – these and many other sensory experiences stimulate green prayer for me, and I am sure you will have your own personal list.

## Sensible Prayer

Stability and contentment are inherent qualities of green prayer. You are happy to be you, in your given circumstances, without constantly eyeing the apparently greener grass on the other side of the fence. It reserves your energy for whatever it is that God is calling you to do, here and now. It is a sober-minded, sensible, matter-of-fact quality. There is no single English word for it, but my Dutch Calvinist friends call it *nuchter*.

## Childlike Trust

Sensing prayer is about the green shoots of fresh beginnings, newness, rebirth and growth.

The childlike qualities of wonderment and unselfconscious gaiety fade and almost disappear as you grow up and become a sophisticated adult. Yet Jesus said that you cannot enter the Kingdom of God unless you welcome it like a little child. One way of bringing to light the hidden child within you is by cultivating green prayer in your life, with its childlike qualities of trust, obedience and lack of anxiety. 'There is no need to worry; but if there is anything you need, pray for it, asking God for it with prayer and thanksgiving.'[12] With that confidence you rest in the Lord like a child, held by God and knowing that you cannot understand all that is happening to you but that you are safe and you are cherished.

Such simple and profound certainty is characteristic of green prayer. It is the kind of certainty shown by Jung when he was asked about his belief in God and replied, 'You can experience God every day . . . I do not take His existence on belief – I *know* that He exists.'[13]

## Extraverted Green Prayer

Extraverted sense perceptions are 'out there'. People who are good at extraverted sensing, particularly ESFP and ESTP types, often say that they like to have a good chat with God. They are pragmatic people who have little patience with theological complications. They relate to God out loud, telling him about their thoughts, their deepest longings, their sorrows and joys. Speaking aloud gives form and clarity to their prayer.

Extraverted sensing types often prefer to externalise their prayer, for instance by drawing and painting, music, sculpture and dance, and by praying in the company of other people.

Green, sensory prayer will not allow you to escape the fact that matter matters. Jesus taught people about God's Kingdom by using material things such as bread, wine, oil, seeds, trees, fields, stones, doorways, water, pearls, coins, fish. Physical place for prayer is important, too. For instance, you might find it helpful to arrange a prayer corner in your room with such objects as a Bible, cross, icon, kneeling stool or cushion, flowers, candle, and incense sticks.

Dominic, Francis and Catherine of Siena were among the saints of the Church who experienced a revelation from God while gazing at a crucifix. Many of us are so accustomed to the idea that prayer is inward, mental and verbal that we find it difficult to use external objects in prayer. However, there is nothing idolatrous about praying before an icon, cross or statue. After all, you are not praying *to* those things. You are simply using them to centre your attention on God. Any object that has significance for you can be used in that way, a painting, a mandala, a picture, a piece of stone, a cup of water, a loaf of bread.

## Introverted Green Prayer

Many introverts like to imagine themselves in a particular prayerful place that has special significance for them. So at any time, wherever they may be, they can place themselves in, say, a favourite chapel or a much-loved place of pilgrimage. That is an introverted sensing gift.

Introverted green prayer pays attention to God through an inner awareness of sensory impressions. It uses the five senses in the mind. People with a good ability for introverted sensing, particularly the ISFJ and ISTJ types, can remember with clarity and vivid detail. They often have excellent recall of conversations, people and events. They 'see with the mind's eye' and sometimes have photographic memories.

Mental images often appear during introverted green prayer, sometimes with extraordinary clarity as if on a screen inside your head. For instance, using the 'application of the senses' as suggested by St Ignatius, you might visualise a scene from the Gospels and then place yourself there in the crowd. You can feel in your hand the stone that you are about to hurl at the woman taken in adultery. You are pouring the precious oil over Christ's feet, or touching his robe and listening to him speaking to you, or dancing at the wedding feast in Cana, or standing with Mary at the foot of the Cross.

## Green Prayer and Church Leaders

A national newspaper accused church leaders of underestimating 'the importance that simple but readily comprehensible images play in reducing great religious mysteries to concepts which ordinary mortals can come to terms with.'[14]

Most ordinary mortals, probably as many as three out of four, are sensing types. For them readily comprehensible images are vital – stories, pictures, religious objects, the concrete, the visible, the audible, the tangible. Sensing people communicate factually with clarity and directness and they stick to the point. S types on the whole dislike complexities, ambiguities, paradoxes, metaphors and flowery language.

Most religious leaders, however, are to be found among the minority intuitive-preferring people, the –NF–s or –NT–s. Their religious symbols are intellectual, conceptual, abstract and philosophical. They dislike any attempt to simplify complexities and mysteries. Not only for their own sakes but for the sake of those they lead and influence, they have an obligation to open themselves to the childlike simplicity and humility of green prayer.

## Intuitive Prayer

### Yellow Prayer – The Intuitive Gift

| Dominant iNtuition | Auxiliary iNtuition | Tertiary iNtuition | Inferior iNtuition |
|---|---|---|---|
| ENFP | ENFJ | ESFJ | ESFP |
| ENTP | ENTJ | ESTJ | ESTP |
| INFJ | INFP | ISFP | ISFJ |
| INTJ | INTP | ISTP | ISTJ |

If N is dominant or auxiliary in your type, you will probably find yellow prayer is the way you most naturally relate to God.

If N is your tertiary or inferior, the intuitive function can be unpredictable and unruly. You therefore need to get in touch with it in a positive, deliberate, playful and prayerful way. You may benefit from giving special attention to yellow prayer, particularly in the second half of life when you will probably find that you are increasingly drawn to it anyway.

## The Yellow Brick Road

Lyman Frank Baum's fantasy story, *The Wonderful Wizard of Oz*, tells how Dorothy and her little dog are carried up by a whirlwind from the Kansas prairies to the land of Oz. With three strange companions and many adventures along the way she follows the Yellow Brick Road to the Emerald City to meet the Wizard of Oz. All four of them have special requests to make of the Wizard. The Cowardly Lion wants courage, the Tin Woodman wants a heart, the Scarecrow longs for a brain and Dorothy wants to go back to Kansas.

During the journey along the Yellow Brick Road the very thing that each of the travellers is longing for is revealed. It becomes clear that the Lion who regards himself as a coward is really very brave; that the Tin Woodman has great compassion; and that it is always the Scarecrow, who thinks he has no brains, who comes up with solutions to the problems that they meet along the way.

The yellow brick road of intuitive prayer leads us into the adventures and possibilities that God has in store for us, and it also releases the latent potential in us. So often we discover in yellow prayer that what we want from God is what he has already given us.

## Musing with God

One aspect of intuitive prayer is full of fantasy, symbols and associations. I think of this way of using intuitive perception in prayer as musing with God. You open yourself to all the possibilities that God wants to show you. You see visions and dream dreams.

It is not a T type of thinking, in which you are actively working things out. Rather, it is being with God thoughtfully. That N, as distinct from T, kind of thought is described by D.H. Lawrence as 'the welling up of unknown life into consciousness . . . gazing on the face of life and reading what can be read . . . man in his wholeness, wholly attending.'[15]

## Freewheeling Prayer

This prayer is bright yellow, sunny, stimulating, provocative, vigorous and hopeful. It is like wandering along the beach, waiting to see what the sea washes up. Much of it is useless flotsam and jetsam. Ideas float around, images come and go, and now and again in this loose and relaxed freewheeling way of communing with God (and this prayer must always be 'with God', not ego-centred daydreaming) significant perceptions occur. 'Sometimes I'm blessed with wonderful brief flashes of insight', someone said to me, describing this intuitive musing prayer. People come to mind. Things to be done come to mind. It is prayer of intuitive association guided by the Holy Spirit.

A good example of intuitive association is Wilfrid Wilson Gibson's poem 'The Icecart' in which the sight of ice triggers off a fantastic train of connected images:

> Perched on my city office-stool
> I watched with envy, while a cool
> And lucky carter handled ice. . .
> And I was wandering in a trice,
> Far from the grey and grimy heat
> Of that intolerable street,
> O'er sapphire berg and emerald floe,
> Beneath the still, cold ruby glow
> Of everlasting Polar night,
> Bewildered by the queer half-light,
> Until I stumbled, unawares,
> Upon a creek where big white bears
> Plunged headlong down with flourished heels,
> And floundered after shining seals
> Through shivering seas of blinding blue. . .[16]

In yellow prayer, when you are using your intuitive perception, you will often experience similar imaginative leaps from the springboard of everyday events. In this prayer God uses your intuitive ability to show, teach, remind, encourage and inspire you.

## Butterfly Prayer

If you have a butterfly mind that flits from one thought to another, this kind of prayer will be familiar to you. As a dominant intuitive, I find it a happy way of prayer, invigorating and wonderfully energising. However, I recognise my own type bias and I know that many Christians can be quite alarmed or even threatened by yellow prayer. They find this kind of prayer disturbing and distracting.

Though it is cheerful and warm, yellow is not a very popular colour. People often say they like it but could not live with it. It is a good colour, therefore, for a way of perceiving and praying that is widely admired but for practical purposes not preferred by most people.

Those whose N function is preferred will naturally and easily follow their way along the significant thoughts and discard the rest. Perhaps many of the so-called distractions in prayer that sensing types often complain about are in fact intuitive perceptions, shafts of yellow prayer trying to break through. If so, and they can be welcomed and drawn into prayer rather than resisted, they may open up an entirely new dimension of prayer for S types.

## Apophatic Contemplation

Another kind of yellow prayer – perhaps it is more white with a touch of yellow – is deeply contemplative. There the leap-frogging intuitive perceptions are stilled and the mind is emptied of all images. As in green prayer, you are sitting quietly, doing nothing, simply being with God. However, it is anything but clearly focused in present reality. Here you are caught up in a timeless, unfocused awareness of God. It is the apophatic, imageless prayer of mystical union with the incomprehensible Other. Its intention is summed up in these words:

> Lord, I offer what I am
> to what You are.
> I stretch up to You in desire
> my attention on You alone.

> I cannot grasp you
> > explain You
> > describe You
> Only cast myself into the depths
> > of your mystery
> Only let Your love pierce the
> > cloud of my unknowing

> Let me forget all but You
> You are what I long for
> You are my chiefest good
> You are my eager hope
> You are my allness.

> In the glimpses of Your eternity
> > Your unconditional Freedom
> > Your unfailing Wisdom
> > Your perfect Love
> I am humble and worshipping
> warming to love and hope

waiting and available
for your Will, dear Lord.[17]

In this palest of yellow apophatic prayer you empty your mind and enter the cloud of unknowing to apprehend the transcendent God. It is a relationship with One who can never be fully known or described, who is so much more than any image you can ever imagine, whose name and nature is a mystery encompassing an infinity of possibilities. It rejects all that might impose limits and boundaries on God. It is the prayer of quiet that transcends physical realities and allows God to take you beyond the here-and-now to Utopia, which literally means 'Nowhere'.

It is difficult to put such an ineffable encounter into words. I once heard two INFP types talking together about the contemplative experience. One said that it is like 'Floating in the sea of God's love', and the other said that it feels like 'Swimming in the tide of God'. Evelyn Underhill said that the contemplative 'suddenly feels that he knows it, in the complete, vital, but indescribable way in which one knows a friend. More, that through it hints are coming to him of mightier, nameless things . . . from the transcendental world.'[18] For St Bernard contemplation was 'the soul's true unerring intuition', and 'the unhesitating apprehension of truth'.[19]

## Holy Restlessness

Yellow prayer is often disturbing and unsettling. It produces a sense of Divine discontent and an insatiable hunger for God. Green prayer is steady and routine. Yellow prayer is impatient with routines and procedures. It happens any time, anywhere, often in great sunbursts of enthusiasm followed by slack times. It is then that the regularity of green prayer becomes a vital anchor for the intuitive. The two ways, green and yellow, need each other and must be held together in creative tension.

## Extraverted Yellow Prayer

Extraverted intuition scans the outer world like a mine sweeper, picking up any perceptions that have special meaning. So extraverted yellow prayer is always seeking to find new and ingenious ways of co-operating with God to transform the world into God's

Kingdom. The inner vision alone is not enough, unless it can be turned into external reality. Extraverted intuitives, especially ENFJs, have described this to me as a yearning desire to be used by God, a longing to extend healing arms around the world.

Extraverted intuitive prayer may be painted or expressed in clay, offered in music, dance, dialogue or drama. Many people find that writing a spiritual journal is a helpful way of meeting the intuitive God 'out there'. In these and many other ways your insights are given external expression.

## Introverted Yellow Prayer

The apophatic contemplation mentioned above, in which you are totally absorbed in a state of emptiness and almost non-being, out of touch with time and place, is essentially introverted. So also is the fantasy prayer in which we pay attention to God through freewheeling intuitive association. The Australian aboriginal 'Walkabout' is one image of introverted yellow prayer, a long, solitary and contemplative journey into the mysterious interior wasteland.

## The Model for All Prayer?

Introverted intuitive prayer is often looked up to, especially by extraverted sensing types, who think of it as mystical or deeply contemplative. Spiritual writers, ancient and modern, tend to be introverted intuitive types themselves. Very often they seem to present what I call yellow prayer as the model for all prayer.

It is certainly a lovely way of prayer, but it is not the only one. It is not even, for many people, the best one. We have to beware not only of type bias, but also of outward appearance which can be very deceptive. The popular image of someone 'deep in prayer' is of a person in absorbed introversion. It is not of someone singing or dancing or peacemaking or caring for the distressed. The absorbed stillness and the vacant gaze of the introverted yellow pray-er is not necessarily more profound or qualitatively superior to the extravert's unselfconscious 'love in action' prayer that is going on in the midst of the noise and demands of work or family. It is merely different. For a holistic prayer life, all the colours are in your palette to be used appropriately as ways of responding to God.

# The Judging Functions: Active Prayer

Blue prayer and red prayer together encompass the human way of responding to God by acts of will. Through them we co-operate with God by our decisions, resolutions and actions. Blue and red prayer, whether introverted or extraverted, are active ways of praying by which we shape our lives and order our world to imitate Christ and bring about his Kingdom.

## Thinking Prayer

### Blue Prayer – The Thinking Gift

| Dominant Thinking | Auxiliary Thinking | Tertiary Thinking | Inferior Thinking |
|---|---|---|---|
| ESTJ | ESTP | ESFP | ESFJ |
| ENTJ | ENTP | ENFP | ENFJ |
| ISTP | ISTJ | ISFJ | ISFP |
| INTP | INTJ | INFJ | INFP |

If T is dominant or auxiliary in your type, you will probably find blue prayer is the way you most naturally relate to God.

If T is your tertiary or inferior, the thinking function can be unpredictable and unruly. You therefore need to get in touch with it in a positive, deliberate, playful and prayerful way. You may benefit from giving special attention to blue prayer, particularly in the second half of life when you will probably find that you are increasingly drawn to it anyway.

Many long for intimacy with God – to experience God. It is to be hoped that the famous social psychologist Abraham Maslow was wrong when he noted nearly thirty years ago that religious

institutions seem to be led by 'non-peakers' (those who themselves have not had religious experience) trying to teach other
'non-peakers' about 'peak experiences.' Church leaders need to
be men and women of prayer who can direct others along the
path of prayer.[1]

F types, and specifically INF– types, often give the impression that
genuine prayer must include a sense of intimacy. You have not
really encountered God, they suggest, unless you have had a private, mystical experience of the kind known only to Maslow's
'peakers'.

T-preferring Christians can feel spiritually inadequate because
they have never had a 'peak experience'. Whenever someone (and
it is usually a clergyman) says to me, 'I try to pray, but I cannot
honestly remember ever having a genuine experience of God', I
am fairly certain that the person speaking to me is a Thinking type.

Ts are critical about themselves. They are objectively honest
and distrust emotional reactions especially in religious matters.
Their approach to God is more likely to be head-to-head than
heart-to-heart. All too often they have been told that their T
approach does not qualify as real prayer. For instance, one popular
writer on prayer offers his readers

some very simple theories that I follow in my own prayer life
and in guiding others in the matter of prayer – That prayer is to
be made less with the head than with the heart. In fact the
sooner it gets away from the head and from thinking the more
enjoyable and the more profitable it is likely to become.[2]

Blue prayer counterbalances that biased F attitude by insisting
that prayer does not have to be affective. Nor does it have to be
enjoyable. Prayer as thinking is valid. Prayer as confrontation is
real prayer.

That must be proclaimed loudly and often for the sake of T-
preferring people. F types, too, need to hear it so that by turning to
hard-edged, tough-thinking blue prayer they can when necessary
counter their inclination to ignore unpleasant truths and rely too
much on cosy prayer and warm feelings. The rigorous honesty of
Thinking prayer also serves to safeguard the faith against super-
stition.

Blue prayer gazes on the truth, which is how the great Christian
thinker St Thomas Aquinas defined contemplation. It is a rational
relationship with God that loves to be stretched to the limits of

argument and logic, to follow thoughts to the place where thought runs out. It is opening your mind to the mind of the infinite. It searches for truth and is always asking 'Why?' Blue prayer celebrates the gift of knowledge and the ability to meet God with the mind through Scripture and the study of theology.

## Polemical Prayer

One of my colleagues, an INTJ type, finds the blue way of prayer suits his personality admirably. 'I am a natural sceptic', he told me. 'I came to faith by arguing with God and losing, just as Paul did. My spirituality began when my arguments ran out.'

Whereas F types will select Scripture verses that give them words of encouragement and comfort, T types will approach their Bible reading with the cool, open-minded detachment that characterises blue prayer. 'The Bible is argumentative and annoying,' says my colleague. 'It's a polemical book, and certainly doesn't make for peace and harmony. Take Psalm 37, for instance – "I have been young, and now am old: and yet I have not seen the righteous forsaken, or his children begging bread." Rubbish! Job was written against that. And take Paul, in Romans. He *needs* someone to argue with, and so he sets up a straw man and directs his arguments at that. Prayer is like that for me. I hate shallow spirituality, just as I hate shallow preaching. Prayer, liturgy and sermons should be stretching. I do try to touch the emotions in myself, the love and the anger, but I find that I can't do that without thinking about it. So my prayer is always discursive.'

## Confrontational Prayer

Edward Schillebeekx has pointed out that the East Asian religions of Hinduism, Jainism, Buddhism and Taoism are primarily religions of inwardness with no confrontation between human and divine, whereas the prophetic West Asian religions, Judaism, Christianity and Islam, experience God as personal.[3] The God of those religions continually challenges human beings, who are responsible and must give account of their stewardship.

God meets you face to face in Thinking prayer. He makes demands on your life, for integrity, responsibility, justice, righteousness, freedom. Blue prayer cannot be divorced from ethical action towards God's Kingdom of justice on earth. In this prayer God is constantly confronting you as a steward of his creation and as a servant of his people. So the practice of blue prayer will never let you forget that God calls you to responsible concern for social justice and that political awareness and activity are imperatives for Christians.

In blue prayer sin is never understated but is seen as it really is – vile transgression against the all-holy God, unloving and culpable failure to obey the moral order of God. God's anger is as personal and as real as his love.

In blue prayer you also confront God, pouring out your complaints before him and telling him all your trouble.[4] Over forty of the psalms are cries of complaint against God.

> How much longer will you forget me, Yahweh? For ever?
> How much longer will you hide your face from me?
> How much longer must I endure grief in my soul,
> and sorrow in my heart by day and by night?
> How much longer must my enemy have the upper hand of
> me?
> Look and answer me, Yahweh my God. . .
> But I for my part rely on your love, Yahweh.[5]

> And at the ninth hour Jesus cried out with a loud voice, 'Eloi, Eloi, lama sabachthani?' which means, 'My God, my God, why have you deserted me?'[6]

Job angrily challenges God to explain himself. So you too can face God in blue prayer with all the pain and hatred, violence and injustice, all that offends your sense of fairness and compassion. There is nothing in the world that you cannot bring to God in prayer.

In Giovanni Guareschi's stories, after furious battles with Peppone, the Communist mayor, the priest Don Camillo has a habit of venting his anger in church before the crucified Christ – who usually gives him little sympathy. For F types, whose Shadow personalities often carry much unresolved anger, this blue prayer of confrontation with God is liberating and healing. After all, how can you love someone you can never be angry with?

## Extraverted Blue Prayer

In its extraverted form, blue prayer embodies Amos 5:24, 'Let justice flow like water and integrity like an unfailing stream'. It is the Holy Spirit, the Spirit of Truth at work in your individual and communal lives giving you the energy and the will to make the world a truthful place. That may take the form of prayer as prophetic action by which you relate your faith to the challenges of political and social ideas and problems, speaking up, joining pressure groups, working for peace and justice in the world. Extraverted T prayer is righteousness in action.

The revolutionary struggle of thousands of base communities in Central and South America is extraverted blue prayer, in which Christians are studying the Scriptures, participating in the sacraments and empowering one another in a communal effort under God to cause political change. The civil rights movement in the United States, with its strong Christian motivation, was blue prayer in action, helping to create a society that more nearly reflected the values of God's Kingdom.

The famous preacher Phillips Brooks, rector of Trinity Episcopal Church in Boston, called attention to the visible, embodied character of extraverted blue prayer:

> Only a person can truly utter a person. Only from a character can a character be echoed. You might write it all over the skies that God was just, but it would not burn there. It would be, at best, only a bit of knowledge; never a Gospel; never something which it would gladden men's hearts to know. That comes only when a human life, capable of a justice like God's, made just by God, glows with his justice in the eyes of men, a candle of the Lord.

## Introverted Blue Prayer

When you love the Lord your God with all your mind, praying with your intellect, wrestling with a portion of Scripture as Jacob wrestled with God,[7] you are engaged in introverted blue prayer.

Some T-preferring friends have told me that they pray with the daily newspaper or with a TV documentary, relating what they are reading and seeing to the God of their Christian faith.

One said, 'I have what I call a Rescue Book. I pray by writing in it to God, often in an argumentative way, and I put all the things there that I don't understand. For intercessory prayer I have photos at the back of my rescue book. I look at those photos, think about the people in them, and catch them up with God in my inner world.'

A form of introverted blue prayer is a ruthless examination of your conscience, trying before God to analyse your life dispassionately and with complete honesty, and then to discern where you are falling short of the best that God wants of you.

## Blue and Green Prayer

The judging functions in prayer will always be informed by one or other of the perceiving functions, S or N. The green sensing prayer together with the blue thinking prayer, the ST combination, will guide you towards a tough-minded, hard-edged spirituality that is disciplined, specific and detailed. ST prayer is well constructed and balanced. It has about it a Benedictine stability and rhythm of work, worship, study and recreation.

However, ST prayer that is not balanced with the yellow and red ways of prayer can be in danger of slipping into rationalism. Reason then takes over in an arrogant and unhelpful way, so that you come to think that God can be explained or even proved intellectually, with no need for divine revelation.

## Blue and Yellow Prayer

When blue thinking prayer is combined with the yellow intuitive forms of prayer, the resulting NT combination may open you to new insights to God's truth and a visionary global grasp of God's purposes. The NT prayer is never complacent but always trying to push the boundaries out in relationship with God.

The possible danger of that blue and yellow NT combination is that you will take yourself altogether too seriously and burden yourself with inappropriate disciplines. If you pay no attention to the green and red ways of prayer, and make no effort to bring them into a holistic harmony with your blue and yellow preferences, you could eventually slip into that kind of heresy that renounces or despises God's good gifts for the sake of mastery in your spiritual life. The unbalanced NT way of prayer can lead to extreme and inappropriate asceticism.

## Loving Discipline

Blue prayer is an act of love in the T sense. It is willed, unemotional and disciplined. You offer it because it is 'meet and right so to do'. Your worship and devotion is God's due and certainly does not depend on how you feel!

T types often react strongly against what they are inclined to call the 'happy-clappy certainties' of charismatic worship. Yet the inferior or tertiary F does sometimes lead Ts to seek 'peak experiences' in the form of unthinking emotionalism. Occasionally you will see yourself or others, who in normal life are intelligent, discriminating Ts, being swept along by unthinking, shallow emotionalism in acts of worship which require that brains are left at the church door.

Nevertheless, charismatic and other forms of Feeling prayer can be enormously helpful for T types who want to bring their whole selves, hearts and minds, in love to God. The release from intellectual critical thinking which is offered in the gift of praying in tongues, for instance, can be the Holy Spirit's way of freeing you for new life in Christ. Similarly the warm and unselfconscious freedom of a well balanced charismatic Christian community can be wonderfully liberating for T types.

The objective, willed, disciplined love of the cool blues and the subjective, feeling love of the warm reds are both there in you to be brought together in synthesis, not for one to be rejected in favour of the other.

## Feeling Prayer

### Red Prayer – The Feeling Gift

| Dominant Feeling | Auxiliary Feeling | Tertiary Feeling | Inferior Feeling |
|---|---|---|---|
| ESFJ | ESFP | ESTP | ESTJ |
| ENFJ | ENFP | ENTP | ENTJ |
| ISFP | ISFJ | ISTJ | ISTP |
| INFP | INFJ | INTJ | INTP |

If F is dominant or auxiliary in your type, you will probably find red prayer is the way you most naturally relate to God.

If F is your tertiary or inferior, the feeling function can be unpredictable and unruly. You therefore need to get in touch with it in a positive, deliberate, playful and prayerful way. You may benefit from giving special attention to red prayer, particularly in the second half of life when you will probably find that you are increasingly drawn to it anyway.

'My father, who was described by one who knew him as "granite on fire" and was certainly never regarded as sentimental, could not speak of the love of God without tears.'[8] Some of the qualities of red prayer are in that description of William Temple's father. There is nothing sentimental, soft and simpering about it. It has nothing in common with the mawkish saints depicted in some Victorian stained glass windows. It is 'granite on fire'.

The colour of fire and blood is well suited to a prayer-relationship with God that has the warmth and passion of red prayer. It can be gentle and tender, or strong and powerful, yet move you to tears.

Red prayer essentially stirs the heart while blue prayer stirs the mind. Red prayer brings spiritual gifts of love, joy and peace while blue prayer brings gifts of insight, wisdom and knowledge. One is affective, the other speculative. Holistic prayer will hold both together, not in opposition but in synthesis.

From the palest pink to the most flaming of red prayer, God is experienced in the heart, in a personal and intimate relationship. From the desert fathers of the fourth century to modern day charismatics affective spirituality has been taught and practised as central to the Christian's experience of God.

### God Our Mother

> Mother, I love you so.
> Said the child, I love you more than I know.
> She laid her head on her mother's arm,
> And the love between them kept them warm.[9]

The male imagery of God produced by the patriarchal culture of the Bible has to be complemented by the female image of God. Both images are there in the tradition and both the male and female aspects of humanity are there in each person. In the Shadow of every man is an unconscious feminine figure, which Jung called the 'anima'. Its counterpart, the 'animus' is the hidden male personality in the Shadow of every woman. Male and female, both are created in the image of God.

F prayer may help men, in particular, to recognise and discriminate positively against the patriarchal and androcentric assumptions in our spirituality. God is not only Father, King, Lord and Master. God is also Mother, travailing in birth and nurturing her children. God is like a pregnant woman in the pangs of giving birth:

> I groan like a woman in labour,
> I suffocate, I stifle.[10]

God is fiercely protective of you and will no more forget you, or lose you, or allow you to be hurt, than a mother will her child.

> For Zion was saying, 'Yahweh has abandoned me,
> the Lord has forgotten me'.
> Does a woman forget her baby at the breast,
> or fail to cherish the son of her womb?
> Yet even if these forget,
> I will never forget you.[11]

God comforts you as a mother comforts her child.

> At her breast will her nurslings be carried
> and fondled in her lap.
> Like a son comforted by his mother
> will I comfort you.[12]

In the year 1413 Julian of Norwich received from God sixteen revelations of the love of God which she called 'Showings'. A central feature of those Showings was the revelation of the Holy Trinity as our Father-Mother God.

And so I saw that God rejoices that he is our Father, and God rejoices that he is our Mother, and God rejoices that he is our true spouse, and that our soul is his beloved wife. . . As truly as God is our Father, so truly is God our Mother, and he revealed that in everything, and especially in these sweet words where he says: I am he; that is to say: I am he, the power and goodness of fatherhood; I am he, the wisdom and lovingness of motherhood; I am he, the light and the grace which is all blessed love; I am

he, the Trinity; I am he, the unity; I am he, the great supreme
goodness of every kind of thing; I am he who makes you to love;
I am he who makes you to long; I am he, the endless fulfilling of
all true desires.[13]

It is this God of wisdom and lovingness to whom we relate in the
red prayer of the Feeling function. Red prayer is to the God who
loves us into life, the God for whom we long, the endless fulfilling
of desire, the God to whom we say, 'our hearts are restless until
they find their rest in Thee.'
 Jesus, too, is revealed to Julian in his female aspect.

But our true Mother Jesus, he alone bears us for joy and for
endless life, blessed may he be. So he carries us with him in
love. . . The mother can give her child to suck of her milk, but
our precious Mother Jesus can feed us with himself, and does,
most courteously and most tenderly, with the blessed sacrament,
which is the precious food of true life.[14]


## Compassionate Prayer

Red prayer is the uniting of our compassion with God's compassion. The God whose name and nature is Love is not the
'unmoved Mover' of philosophers, but the God revealed as the
Suffering Servant. God grieves with you. God gives you the gift of
tears and weeps with you. God longs for your love and pierces
your heart with love.
 In red prayer you are in communion with God who says to you,
'I will listen, for I am full of pity'.[15] When your heart is moved with
compassion, or when you see compassion in others, it is always a
sign of Christ's indwelling. All human experience of compassion,
and indeed of goodness in any form, is a manifestation of the Holy
Spirit at work and is a part of what I call red prayer.
 Red prayer relates to our Mother Jesus who wept, who was
tender and gentle, who forgave, and who cried over Jerusalem,
'How often have I longed to gather your children, as a hen gathers
her chicks under her wings, and you refused!'[16]

## Intimate Prayer

Fs easily feel hurt and they take pain and guilt on themselves. In red prayer those feelings are acknowledged before the God who understands, who affirms and who lifts the burdens you may be carrying needlessly.

There is often a spontaneous intimacy about red prayer, a sudden surge of love, a lift of the heart. 'I often feel like giving God a hug', I heard someone say. It is prayer of praise, thanksgiving and sheer delight in the goodness of God and the gifts of God. It is, as Thomas à Kempis put it, a familiar friendship with Jesus.

Your pictures of God in red prayer will often be intimate ones, and your prayer may be focused on the person of Jesus, thought of as your Brother, Shepherd, Friend and Companion on the Way.

## Prayer of Forgiveness

Red prayer is affective. It touches the emotions and longs for harmony. In the language of red prayer, sin is disharmony with God and with other people. It breaks relationship, destroys trust and offends love.

In red prayer, however, we learn to forgive and to receive forgiveness. 'Our love is not to be just words or mere talk, but something real and active.' Only then can we quieten our consciences 'because God is greater than our conscience and he knows everything.'[17] The red prayer-relationship demands that your heart is right before God.

## Prayer of the Heart

Red prayer can never be formal or merely routine. It is heart-felt and full of life. 'He who believes in me, as the scripture has said, "Out of his heart shall flow rivers of living water." '[18] It is a love relationship with One who discloses the purposes of the heart, who knows you inside out and cares for you more than you could ever know.

In red prayer you incline your heart to One who withholds nothing from you that is really for your good. You can harden your heart against God, but God's heart is never hardened against you. 'We teach what scripture calls: *the things that no eye has seen and no ear has heard, things beyond the mind of man, all that God has prepared for those who love him.*'[19]

## Introverted Red Prayer

An introvert whose dominant function is F said, 'My feeling is inside, where I live'. Introverted Fs feel very deeply but the strength of their feelings may not be apparent to others. Their prayer may be powerfully felt but rarely shown. In their deepest hearts the word of God is living and active, discerning their secret emotions and thoughts.[20]

They will often spend considerable time alone in intercessory prayer for specific people and special causes, praying for the sick and dying, for those who are unloved and lonely, for those caught up in acts of hatred and inhumanity, for those who serve others, and so on. The list can be endless.

In red prayer you place the healing hand of Christ on the brokenness of the world and all your longings for peace and harmony are united with God's redeeming love in Christ. These heart-felt longings are often inexpressible. In red prayer you may simply offer your love to God to be used for the sake of others.

## Extraverted Red Prayer

In extraverted red prayer you respond to God in practical acts of care and loving service to others. That may take the form of a symbolic action. For instance, a friend told me about her parish priest's care for a parishioner who had been ordered to give up smoking for health reasons. The priest promptly gave up smoking himself to 'be with' his parishioner in that effort to break the habit of a lifetime.

Praying with others, especially in intercession and through the laying-on of hands for healing, is a powerful way of expressing red prayer.

## Red and Green Prayer

When the red Feeling function is informed in prayer by Sensing perception, the resultant SF combination will guide you towards a practical spirituality, expressed in institutionalised forms or in social activity. Many -SF- types offer their prayer to God through practical expressions of love and concern, such as visiting prisoners, running soup kitchens for street people, helping in hospitals.

The possible danger of that red and green combination, if it is allowed to become exaggerated and unbalanced, is a tendency to a kind of puritanical pietism which is suspicious of any intellectual and formalised approach to faith and over-emphasises personal religious experience, particularly a dateable conversion experience.

## Red and Yellow Prayer

Feeling judgement informed by Intuitive perception will guide you towards a universal spirituality that is focused on possibilities for people. NF spirituality has a warm enthusiasm about it, and a desire to cooperate with God to draw the fullest potential out of every person and every situation. For -NF- people a ministry of listening, perhaps counselling or helping with marital problems, potential suicides or drug addicts, may be their way of putting red prayer into action in the world.

The danger of the NF combination, when exaggerated and out of balance, is that it can lead to an impractical idealistic spirituality, a kind of quietism which merely wants to withdraw to a private 'spiritual' existence unrelated to the concerns or demands of worldly affairs.

*Red, blue, green and yellow, all prayer is God's initiative.*
*Your prayer is always response to God.*
*There is no one correct way of responding to God in prayer.*
*Your prayer is a living, growing, developing relationship with God.*
*You will pray in different ways at different times*
*and at different stages of life.*
*You have the green and yellow, blue and red*
*gifts of prayer in all the colours of the rainbow*
*to show your covenant love for God*
*and receive God's covenant love for you.*

# Notes

## Chapter 1: Companionship with God

1. John 4:34 (RSV).
2. John 14:16.
3. Martin Buber.
4. Luke 24:13–35.
5. Psalm 42:1,2.
6. William Cowper, 'O For a Closer Walk With God'. Included in *The English Hymnal* (OUP, 1933) and various other editions.
7. Galatians 4:19.
8. John 10:10.
9. Luke 10:41–2.
10. *Myers-Briggs Type Indicator* is a registered trademark, and MBTI is a trademark of Consulting Psychologists Press, Inc.

## Chapter 2: Your Personality – A Model

1. Ken Rawling, *Introducing the Cambridge Type Inventory* (Rawling Associates, 1992).

## Chapter 3: The Dynamics of Type

1. C.G. Jung, *On Psychic Energy*, in *The Collected Works of C.G. Jung* 8 (Princeton University Press), paras. 60–9. (In future notes the abbreviation *CW* will be used.)

## Chapter 4: Prayer and the Shadow

1. *Book of Common Prayer*, Holy Communion 1662 (OUP).
2. Thomas Merton, *Zen and the Birds of Appetite* (Abbey of Gethsemani Inc., 1968). Quoted in *Modern Spirituality: An Anthology*, edited by John Garvey (DLT, 1986), p. 131.
3. C.G. Jung, *CW* 16, para. 227 quoted in *Jung: Selected Writings*, introduced by Anthony Storr (Fontana Press, 1986), p. 22.
4. C.G. Jung, *Psychology and Religion*, *CW* 11, para. 131.
5. *Psychology and Religion*, *CW* 11, paras. 130–4.

6. Romans 7:15.
7. C.G. Jung, *Two Essays on Analytical Psychology*, *CW* 7, pp. 67, 68.
8. *Psychology and Religion*, *CW* 11, paras. 138–49.
9. John Donne, *Devotions* (OUP).
10. Romans 8:26–7.
11. 1 Peter 3:4.
12. Mark 7:21.
13. C.G. Jung, *The Psychology of Eastern Meditation*, *CW* 17, para. 935.
14. Psalm 1:3.
15. John 4:13–14.
16. C.G. Jung, *General Aspects of Dream Psychology*, *CW* 8, para. 509.
17. Genesis 20:3.
18. 1 Kings 3:5.
19. Matthew 1:20; 2:12–13,19,22.
20. Matthew 27:19.
21. Matthew 6:7–8.
22. Matthew 6:5.
23. Matthew 6:6.
24. Luke 18:9–14.
25. C.G. Jung (quoting Henry Drummond, *The Greatest Thing in the World*) in *Psychology and Religion*, *CW* 11, paras. 130–4.
26. Question put to von Hügel by Rufus Jones, the Quaker.
27. Walter Hilton, *The Ladder of Perfection*, trans. Leo Shirley-Price, (Penguin, 1957), p. 64.
28. *Cloud of Unknowing* (Paulist Press), chapter 14.
29. St Teresa of Avila, *The Interior Castle* (Hodder, 1988).
30. Matthew 23:27,28.
31. Ecclesiastes 7:24.
32. John Donne, Holy Sonnets, XIV *Divine Poems* (OUP).
33. John 8:12.
34. Ephesians 3:16–19.

## Chapter 5: Living Images of God

1. *Alternative Service Book*, Church of England: Rite A, Third Eucharistic Prayer (Clowes SPCK and CUP, 1980).
2. 1 John 3:2.
3. A.M. Allchin, *Christian Believing* (SPCK), p. 140.
4. Ephesians 4:13–16.
5. Wisdom 13:1,5.
6. Psalm 46:10 (RSV).
7. Psalm 94:9.
8. 2 Corinthians 6:2.
9. Jeremiah 32:27.
10. Matthew 19:26.
11. Genesis 18:14.

12. Luke 1:38.
13. Ephesians 1:9–10.
14. 1 John 1:9.
15. Galatians 2:6, Acts 10:34.
16. Romans 11:33–4.
17. Genesis 18:25.
18. Luke 16:15.
19. 2 Corinthians 7:6.
20. 2 Corinthians 1:3 (RSV).
21. 2 Corinthians 1:3.
22. 2 Corinthians 13:11.
23. 1 Corinthians 14:33 (RSV).
24. Mark 10:18.
25. Romans 15:13.
26. Luke 15:7.
27. Psalm 85:10.
28. Romans 11:22.
29. Hebrews 6:17.
30. 1 Kings 18:21.
31. 1 Kings 8:32.
32. Deuteronomy 30:19.
33. Luke 9:62.
34. Genesis 18:24.
35. Nehemiah 9:17.
36. Ephesians 4:13.
37. William Temple, *Readings in St John's Gospel* (Macmillan, 1959), p. xvi.
38. Mark 1:35.
39. Acts 12:12.
40. Mark 14:51.
41. Mark 4:38–9.
42. Mark 5:30.
43. Mark 9:36 and 10:16.
44. Mark 10:21–2.
45. Mark 6:40.
46. Matthew 7:28; 11:1; 13:53; 19:1; 26:1.
47. Matthew 3:12.
48. Matthew 1:22; 2:15,17,23; 4:14; 8:17; 12:17; 13:35; 21:4; 27:9.
49. Luke 7:47.
50. Luke 23:1–25.
51. Luke 15:11–end.
52. Luke 19:1–10.
53. Luke 10:38–42.
54. Luke 23:43.
55. Luke 24:13–35.

56. Luke 5:16.
57. John 1:1–18.
58. William Temple, op. cit., p. xxi.
59. John 1:17–18.
60. 2 Corinthians 4:6 (RSV).
61. John 20:31.

## Chapter 6: Praying Your Way

1. 1 Thessalonians 5:16–18.
2. Bishop John Robinson, *Honest to God* (SCM), p. 100.
3. Richard Foster, *Freedom of Simplicity* (Triangle/SPCK, 1981), p. 80.
4. 2 Timothy 2:3–7.
5. Galatians 5:22–3.
6. 2 Timothy 2:11–13.
7. Meister Eckhart, quoted in *Eckhart's Way*, Richard Woods (DLT, 1987), p. 62.
8. 1 Corinthians 3:7.
9. 2 Corinthians 3:18 (RSV).
10. Philippians 1:6.
11. 2 Corinthians 12:10.
12. 2 Corinthians 12:9.
13. C.G. Jung, *The Development of Personality*, *CW* 17, paras. 284–323.
14. Luke 15:20–1.
15. *The Development of Personality*, *CW* 17, paras. 284–323.
16. Ibid.
17. James 4:8.
18. Found on the body of a Confederate soldier.

## Chapter 7: Holistic Prayer

1. Angelo Spoto, *Jung's Typology in Perspective* (Sigo Press, Boston 1989), p. 12.
2. C.G. Jung, *Psychological Types*, *CW* 6 (1923), para. 895.
3. Lagneus associates the four principal colours with the four temperaments (*Citrinitas* = the choleric temperament, *rubedo* = the sanguine, *albedo* = the phlegmatic, *nigredo* = the melancholic ('Harmonia chemica', *Theatr. chem.*, IV, p. 873).
4. John 1:5.
5. John 1:9.
6. C.G. Jung, *The Archetypes and the Collective Unconscious*, *CW* 9i, p. 332, footnote: 'Statistically, at least, green is correlated with the sensation function', and p. 335: 'yellow = intuition, light blue = thinking, flesh pink = feeling, brown = sensation' and footnote: 'The colour correlated with sensation in the mandalas of other persons is usually green'. 'The four basic functions, which are customarily

represented by the colour quaternio blue-red-yellow-green' (*CW* 14, *Mysterium Coniunctionis*, pp. 286–7).

7. C.G. Jung, *A Psychological Approach to the Trinity*, *CW* 11, p. 189.
8. Philippians 3:10.
9. Thomas Merton, *Zen and the Birds of Appetite* (Abbey of Gethsemani Inc., 1968). Quoted in *Modern Spirituality: An Anthology*, edited by John Garvey (DLT, 1986), p. 131.
10. 1 Corinthians 14:15.
11. Martin Thornton, *English Spirituality* (SPCK, 1963), p. 156.
12. Ibid, p. 49.
13. William of St Thierry, *The Golden Epistle*, Chapter 1.
14. Bruce Duncan, unpublished research project, 1991.

*Chapter 8: The Perceiving Functions: Passive Prayer*

1. e.e. cummings, *Selected Poems 1923–1958* (Faber and Faber, 1960), p. 76.
2. Ibid, p. 88.
3. Psalm 96:1,11–12. See also Psalm 148.
4. Psalm 104:31.
5. John 9:26.
6. *Way of a Pilgrim*, trans. Helen Bacovcin (Doubleday, Image, NY 1978), p. 34.
7. R.S. Thomas, *Selected Poems 1946–1968* (Bloodaxe Books Ltd, PO Box 1SN, Newcastle upon Tyne NE99 1SN), p. 88 'The Moor'.
8. Zen saying.
9. Quoted in *Eckhart's Way*, Richard Woods (DLT, 1987), p. 62.
10. Brother Lawrence, *The Practice of the Presence of God* (Burns and Oates, London 1977).
11. 1 John 1:1–2.
12. Philippians 4:6.
13. Interview with Frederick Sands, 1955, in *C.G. Jung: Interviews and Encounters*, eds. William McGuire and R.F.C. Hull (Thames and Hudson, 1978), pp. 249–250.
14. *The Daily Telegraph*, June 1, 1991.
15. D.H. Lawrence, *Last Poems* (Haskell House Pub.).
16. W.W. Gibson, *Friends* (Elkin Matthews, 1916), p. 29.
17. *Oxford Book of Prayer*, ed. George Appleton (OUP, 1985), pp. 56–7.
18. Evelyn Underhill, *Mysticism*, 6th edition (Methuen, 1916), p. 376.
19. St Bernard, *On Consideration*, trans. George Lewis (Clarendon Press, 1908), p. 41.

## Chapter 9: The Judging Functions: Active Prayer

1. Margaret M. Paloma and George H. Gallup Jr, *Varieties of Prayer: A Survey Report* (Trinity Press International, Philadelphia 1991), p. 134.
2. Anthony de Mello, *Sadhana: a Way to God* (Image Books, 1984), p. 7.
3. Edward Schillebeekx, *The Gospel Proclaimed* (SCM, 1983), p. 169.
4. Psalm 142:2.
5. Psalm 13:1–3,5.
6. Mark 15:34.
7. Genesis 32:23–32.
8. William Temple, *Readings in St John's Gospel* (Macmillan, 1959), p. xv.
9. From *The Collected Poems of Stevie Smith* (Allen Lane, 1975).
10. Isaiah 42:14.
11. Isaiah 49:14–15.
12. Isaiah 66:13.
13. *Julian of Norwich: Showings*, trans. Edmund Colledge and James Walsh (Paulist Press, New York 1978), quoted in *Praying with Julian of Norwich*, by Gloria Durka (Saint Mary's Press, Christian Brothers Publications, Winona, Minnesota 1989), pp. 19ff.
14. Ibid.
15. Exodus 22:27.
16. Matthew 23:37.
17. 1 John 3:18,20.
18. John 7:38 (RSV).
19. 1 Corinthians 2:9.
20. Hebrews 4:12.

# Select Bibliography

## Jung and Jungian Psychology

Brome, Vincent. *Jung: Man and Myth*, London: Macmillan 1978; Paladin Books 1980; New York: Atheneum 1978

*Collected Works of C.G. Jung* (cited in footnotes as *CW*), Bollingen Series XX, Volumes 1–18 (Princeton University Press)

Fordham, Frieda. *An Introduction to Jung's Psychology*, London: Pelican 1953

Hannah, Barbara. *Jung: His Life and Work*, New York: G.P. Putnam's Sons 1976

Jung, C.G. *Analytical Psychology: Its Theory and Practice*, London and New York: Ark Paperbacks 1986

   *Memories, Dreams, Reflections*, recorded and edited by Aniela Jaffé; translated by Richard and Clara Winston, New York: Pantheon 1962, 1967; Vintage 1965, 1966. London: Collins and Routledge and Kegan Paul 1963; Fount Paperbacks 1977

*Jung on Elementary Psychology: A Discussion between C.G. Jung and Richard I. Evans*, USA: E.P. Dutton 1976; London: Routledge and Kegan Paul 1979

*Jung: Selected Writings*, introduced by Anthony Storr, Fontana Press 1983

*Man and His Symbols*, edited by Carl Jung, London: Aldus Books 1964; Picador edition, Pan Books 1978

O'Connor, Peter. *Understanding Jung, Understanding Yourself*, New York/Mahwah: Paulist Press 1985

Sharp, Daryl. *Jung Lexicon: A Primer of Terms and Concepts*, Toronto: Inner City Books 1991

Storr, Anthony. *Jung*, London: Fontana Paperbacks 1973

## Jung's Typology

Jung, C.G. *Psychological Types*, London: Routledge 1971, 1991

*Lectures on Jung's Typology*: Marie-Louise von Franz (*The Inferior Function*) and James Hillman (*The Feeling Function*), Dallas, Texas: Spring Publications 1986

Sharp, Daryl. *Personality Types: Jung's Model of Typology*, Toronto: Inner City Books 1987

Spoto, Angelo. *Jung's Typology in Perspective*, Boston: Sigo Press 1989

## Jung and Christianity

Bryant, Christopher, ssje. *Jung and The Christian Way*, London: Darton, Longman and Todd 1983

   *Depth Psychology and Religious Belief*, Mirfield Publications 1972; London: Darton, Longman and Todd 1987

*Carl Jung and Christian Spirituality*, edited by Robert L. Moore, New York/Mahwah: Paulist Press 1988

Clift, Wallace B. *Jung and Christianity: The Challenge of Reconciliation*, New York: Crossroad 1982

Dourley, John P. *The Illness That We Are: A Jungian Critique of Christianity*, Toronto: Inner City Books 1984

White, Victor. *God and the Unconscious*, London: Harvill 1952

## Myers-Briggs Typology

Keirsey, David and Bates, Marilyn. *Please Understand Me: Character and Temperament Types*, distributed by Prometheus Nemesis Book Co., Del Mar, California 1984

Lawrence, Gordon. *People Types and Tiger Stripes: A Practical Guide to Learning Styles*, Gainesville, Florida: Center for Applications of Psychological Type, 2nd edn 1982

Myers, I.B. with Myers, P.B. *Gifts Differing*, Palo Alto, California: Consulting Psychologists Press 1980

Myers, Isabel. *Introduction to Type*, Palo Alto, California: Consulting Psychologists Press 1980

Myers, I.B. and McCaulley, M.H. *Manual: A Guide to the Development of the Myers-Briggs Type Indicator*, Palo Alto, California: Consulting Psychologists Press 1985

## Personality Type and Christian Spirituality

Benner, David G. *Psychotherapy and the Spiritual Quest*, London: Hodder and Stoughton 1989

Bryant, Christopher, ssje. *Prayer and Different Types of People*, Oxford: Society of St John the Evangelist 1980

   *The River Within: The Search for God in Depth*, London: Darton, Longman and Todd 1978

*The Christian Ministry of Spiritual Direction*, edited by David L. Fleming sj, (*Jungian Typology and Christian Spirituality* by Robert A. Repicky csb; *Jungian Types and Forms of Prayer* by Thomas E.

Clarke sj; *The Spiritual Direction of 'Thinking' Types* by Carolyn Osiek rscj), St Louis, Minnesota: Review for Religious 1988

Grant, Harold W., Thompson, Magdala and Clarke, Thomas E. *From Image to Likeness: A Jungian Path in the Gospel Journey*, New York/Ramsey: Paulist Press 1983

Keating, Charles J. *Who we are is How we pray: Matching Personality and Spirituality*, Mystic, Connecticut: Twenty-Third Publications 1987

Michael, Chester P. and Norrisey, Marie C. *Prayer and Temperament: Different Prayer Forms for Different Personality Types*, Charlottesville, Virginia: The Open Door 1984

Osborne, Lawrence and Diana. *God's Diverse People: Personality and the Christian Life*, London: Daybreak, Darton, Longman and Todd 1991

Oswald, Roy M. and Kroeger, Otto. *Personality Type and Religious Leadership*, Washington DC: The Alban Institute 1988

Welch, John, o.carm. *Spiritual Pilgrims: Carl Jung and Teresa of Avila*, New York/Ramsey: Paulist Press 1982

## The Shadow and Mid-Life Spirituality

Brennan, Anne and Brewi, Janice. *Mid-Life Directions: Praying and Playing Sources of New Dynamism*, New York/Mahwah: Paulist Press 1985

Brewi, Janice and Brennan, Anne. *Mid Life: Psychological and Spiritual Perspectives*, New York: Crossroad 1982

Miller, William A. *Make Friends with your Shadow: How to Accept and Use Positively the Negative Side of Your Personality*, Minneapolis: Augsburg 1981

Sanford, John A. *Evil the Shadow Side of Reality*, New York: Crossroad 1987

## Traditions of Spirituality

*Spiritual Traditions for the Contemporary Church*, edited by Robin Maas and Gabriel O'Donnell op, Nashville: Abingdon Press 1990

Thornton, Martin. *English Spirituality*, London: SPCK 1963

*Western Spirituality: Historical Roots, Ecumenical Routes*, edited by Matthew Fox op, Santa Fe, New Mexico: Bear and Company 1981